NOTATIONS and EDITIONS

NOTATIONS and EDITIONS

A Book in Honor of Louise Cuyler

Edited by

EDITH BORROFF
STATE UNIVERSITY OF NEW YORK
AT BINGHAMTON

WM. C. BROWN COMPANY PUBLISHERS
Dubuque, Iowa

Copyright © 1974 by Wm. C. Brown Company Publishers

Library of Congress Catalog Card Number: 72-81623

ISBN 0—697—03543—3

Printed in the United States of America

Dedication

Louise Cuyler has wielded an influence of unusual force and scope in the musical life of a school, a city, and a nation. The purpose of this book is to honor Miss Cuyler in a publication springing from the gratitude and appreciation of her colleagues and students.

Born in Omaha, Nebraska, Louise Cuyler was educated in Omaha. She studied violin from childhood and was an accomplished musician by the time she entered college. After three years she completed her undergraduate degree in violin at the Eastman School of Music. Graduating in 1929, she went directly to the University of Michigan's School of Music as an Instructor in Theory; she continued studying while teaching, and received a master's degree at the University of Michigan in 1933. She has been associated with that institution ever since, becoming Professor of Music in 1953 and Chairman of the Department of Musicology in 1957.

During World War II, Miss Cuyler served with the American Red Cross as program director, club director, and eventually as liaison with Special Services. She was stationed for almost two years on New Caledonia. After the war, she returned to the Eastman School of Music to work in musicology, and received a Ph.D. from that school in 1948. Her thesis, an edition of Heinrich Isaac's *Choralis Constantinus Book III*, is a landmark in Renaissance studies.

It is perhaps as a musicologist and teacher that Louise Cuyler has attained the most commanding stature. Her versatility, intuitive musicianship, lively mind, and pungent analytical skill come into particular focus in guiding the maturing scholar, at which she is unexcelled.

At her home university Louise Cuyler is legendary. No musicologist's career at the University of Michigan School of Music is complete who has not attempted to keep up with the incisive commentary in Church Music to 1600 and Nineteenth-Century Styles and Idioms, and no student has left her guidance without a debt to her wisdom and generosity.

Miss Cuyler's publications include editions of Isaac's *Choralis Constantinus Book III* (The University of Michigan Press, 1950) and the same composer's *Five Polyphonic Masses* (The University of Michigan Press, 1956), a study of *Maximilian I and Music* (Oxford University Press, 1972), and articles on a wide scope of subjects, from Mozart string quartets to modal practice.

Special courses at The University of Michigan adult education centers in Grand Rapids, Flint, and Detroit have brought many people throughout Michigan under Miss Cuyler's influence. Though always known for her Renaissance music courses, Miss Cuyler also presented offerings in twentieth-century and American music, for which subjects she provided an early recognition.

For over two decades Miss Cuyler served as music critic for the *Ann Arbor News*, taking an active role in forming the musical taste of a city long known as an artistic center. As a reviewer she was always penetrating and always constructive, and most often kind (even generous); her reviews could well serve as a textbook for hopeful critics.

Miss Cuyler's service to the American Musicological Society forms a remarkable chapter in the history of that organization. For over twenty years (save for the academic year 1953-1954, when she was a Senior Fulbright Fellow in Belgium), she has variously been on the Council, or served as a Member-at-Large, or, most importantly, for an unprecedented eight terms as National Secretary (1955-1971).

It has been the pleasure of a group of scholars and composers to join in the preparation of this volume in honor of Louise Cuyler. In addition to their cooperation and their work on a subject specifically pointed toward a unified publication, the group undertook the trouble and expense of obtaining the facsimiles, and all have given up their royalties in order to lower the cost of the volume and to send the royalties directly to a scholarship fund, also in her honor, at the University of Michigan.

In further support of this intention, all libraries and publishers have generously waived their customary permission fees. Thanks are due in particular to Miss Alice Tully for her gracious permission to reproduce the holograph of the original construction of the Tema, Opus 13, of Robert Schumann; to the Musée de Mariemont for providing photographs of their manuscript of the entire work, of which the Tema is reproduced here; to the C.F. Peters Corporation for permission to reprint the entire *Fantasy in Two Movements* by Ross Lee Finney (Peters Edition #6063); to J. & W. Chester for permission to reproduce the *Soliloquies* of Paul Cooper (with whom they hold an exclusive contract); from Alfred A. Knopf, Inc., to use the poem "A Sea-Bird" by William Alexander Percy.

Edith Borroff

Contents

1   Medieval Monophonic Song: *Kalenda Maia* by Raimbault de
    Vaqueiras (c. 1155-1205)   1
    Gwynn S. McPeek
    The University of Michigan

2   A Comparison of Two Manuscripts: *Fole acoustumance* (c. 1250)   8
    Hans Tischler
    Indiana University

3   Lyonel Power's *Sanctus* (ca. 1410)   17
    John Reeves White
    Hunter College

4   An Editorial Problem in a Mass by Heinrich Isaac (c. 1450-1517):
    Sanctus and *Benedictus* from *Missa Misericordias Domini*   33
    Gustave Reese
    New York University

5   A German Organ Tablature: *Dies est laetitiae* (c. 1500)   43
    Thomas Warburton
    University of North Carolina at Chapel Hill

6   A Madrigal in Four Voices: *La mia doglia s'avanza* (1613) by
    Pomponio Nenna (c. 1550-c. 1618)   48
    Glenn E. Watkins
    The University of Michigan

7   A Study of Notational and Performance Problems of an Early *Air
    de cour: Je voudrois bien, ô Cloris* (1629) by Antoine Boësset
    (c. 1586-1643)   55
    Albert Cohen
    State University of New York—Buffalo

8   Some Problems of Transcribing Music with Many Sources: The
    Verse Anthem *O Praise God in His Holiness* by Edward Smith   69
    J. Bunker Clark
    University of Kansas

9   English Consort Music: *Fancy and Ayre in G Minor* (c. 1660) by
    John Jenkins (1592-1678)   106
    Robert Austin Warner
    The University of Michigan

10   Some Aspects of Notation in an *Alma Redemptoris Mater*
       (c. 1670) by Marc-Antoine Charpentier (d. 1704)   127
       H. Wiley Hitchcock
       Brooklyn College of the City University of New York

11   Problems in Editing Harpsichord Music: *Suite in D* by
       Ferdinand Tobias Richter (1649-1711)   142
       C. David Harris
       Drake University

12   A Realization by J. C. Heck: An *Affettuoso di molto* by
       Johann Joachim Quantz (1697-1773)   154
       Edward R. Reilly
       Vassar College

13   Robert Alexander Schumann (1810-1856): *Tema*, Opus 13   163
       John L. Kollen
       The University of Michigan

14   Spelling and Intention: A Setting of William Alexander Percy's
       Lyric *A Sea-Bird* (1933) by Irwin Fischer   172
       Edith Borroff
       State University of New York at Binghamton

15   Concerning My *Fantasy in Two Movements* (1958)   182
       Ross Lee Finney
       The University of Michigan

16   A New Notation: *Soliloquies* for Violin and Piano (1971) by
       Paul Cooper   191
       Edith Borroff
       State University of New York at Binghamton

1

Medieval Monophonic Song:
Kalenda Maia
by Raimbault de Vaqueiras (c. 1155-1205)

GWYNN S. McPEEK
THE UNIVERSITY OF MICHIGAN

Of all the songs in the troubadour repertory, probably the best known today, and certainly one of the most pleasing, is the estampida *Kalenda maia* by Raimbault de Vaqueiras. It is beautiful to hear and its structure delightful to contemplate; it is both a microcosm of the artistic world that brought it into being and an archetype of its kind. The *Razo*, or legend about the origin of the piece,[1] tells that some visiting *jongleurs* played a lively dance tune one evening at the court of Boniface I, Marquis of Montferrat, where Raimbault was in service. Boniface is said to have challenged Raimbault to compose one of his characteristically sombre poems to the gay melody, and *Kalenda maia*, according to the legend, was improvised on the spot to answer the challenge. Although the truth of the story is not known (and the elaborate structure of the poem raises doubts), the tale invokes a picture of the setting in which much troubadour music was created and performed; so while it is a unique creation, it is also characteristic of its genre and contains most, if not all, of the general problems to be found in the troubadour repertory as a whole.

The poem is preserved in several manuscripts, only one of which contains the music.[2] All of them come from the late thirteenth or early fourteenth century, or about a hundred years after the piece was composed. Many scholars[3] believe that troubadour songs were transmitted orally until being copied into the sources. Oral tradition explains many of the differences between the sources in spellings, words, idiomatic expressions, and dialect, all reflecting a variety of syntactical usage. When the music of a song exists in several sources, a similar condition prevails there as well.

By the time this piece was written down, the techniques of pitch notation had been in general use about two hundred years, so *Kalenda maia* presents few problems as to pitch. The square notes are copied on staves with a clef sign at the beginning of each staff. The first staff has five lines and all the rest four lines. But if the problems are few in number, they still present considerable difficulty to the person making a modern edition of the piece.

One of the problems is the *plica*. The fourth character in the first staff is a square note with a descending stem on each side, or a *nota plicata*. The plica is an ornamental tone, in this case consisting of a tone sounded after the written pitch on the degree below it and using the same syllable of text as the written pitch. The plica here is similar to a short passing note on *g* between the written *a* and the next written note on *f*. Although the pitch of the plica is clear enough, precisely how it was performed is a matter of conjecture. It is, perhaps, a greater problem to the performer than to the editor, for it can be written thus: ♩ ♪ , or it can be incorporated into the time of the ornamented note thus: ♩. ♪ .

The next problem is a complex one which plagues the editors of all medieval and renaissance music: how long are chromatic changes valid, and to what extent should they be added when they are not written? It was common at the time *Kalenda maia* was copied and for a long time thereafter to put a chromatic change quite some distance ahead of the note it modified. The source shows a flat in the first staff above the fifth note, although the *b* to which it refers is the eighth

Kalenda maia. **The only source with the music. Paris: Bibliothèque Nationale, f. fr. ms. 22543, folio 62 recto. column 2.**

character. The second staff shows a flat above the fifth note from the end, while the *b* to which it refers comes two notes later. In the transcription of this piece, the two flats in the source are put immediately in front of the note each one modifies.

As to how long the flats are meant to apply, the picture is less clear. Generally, but with many exceptions, a chromatic flat is valid for the remainder of the staff in which it appears or until there is a full stop (that is, a bar line connecting all the lines of the staff) at the close of a major section—whichever comes first. The semistop or breath mark, a shorter vertical line which connects some (but not all) of the lines of the staff, ordinarily does not cancel a chromatic. How long

the flats are valid in *Kalenda maia* depends in great part on whether one views as full stops or as half stops all the vertical strokes that mark the ends of musical phrases and poetic lines. Two of the strokes are very faint and although they can be seen in the manuscript, they are almost invisible in the photograph. The first of these occurs in the first staff after the fifth character of the piece, above the "a" of *maya*. The second is in the fifth staff after the second note, above the word *vos*. If one decides that the vertical strokes are full stops, then the bar line after the tenth note in the top staff cancels the flat, and the two *b*'s which come after it in the top staff can be natural. However, if one decides the strokes are semistops, then the flat is valid throughout the top staff and the last two b's are flatted. The transcription presented here considers them to be breath marks and therefore the flats are continued and are placed above the notes in question since they represent editorial additions based on opinion. However, once an interpretation of the vertical strokes is made, that choice, whichever it is, permeates all the rest of the piece, for there are five more *b's* to be considered.

The last four characters in the first staff, which contain the two *b's* in question, are repeated as the first four characters of the third staff where there is no flat, although the two passages fulfill the same function in the music and in the poetry. If one has chosen to flat them in the top staff (considering the strokes to be breath marks), then it is reasonable to expect that those at the beginning of the third staff should be flatted also, regardless of the absence of a flat there. In this case editorial flats are required above the notes as the transcription has put them. If, however, one has chosen to call the strokes full stops, then there is no need for editorial flats in either instance but he will have to accept vascillation between $b^\flat$ and $b^\natural$ in the course of this short melody.

Still another interpretation is possible for the last four notes of the first staff and the first four of the third. The melodic pattern here involves the notes *a-b-c'-b-a*. A widely-held opinion states that when a melody passes through *b* on the way from *a* to *c'*, *b* should be natural; but when the *b* is sounded on the way from *c'* down to *a*, it should be flatted. Following this opinion the two passages in question would each be rendered: *a-b$^\natural$-c'-b$^\flat$-a*.

Three more *b's* are still to be considered. The first is in staff three, the third character from the end, while the others are in staff four, the sixth and seventh characters. Here too it is possible to choose either the flat or the natural *b* and support one's choice with considerable argument. From one point of view, since there is no flat in either staff three or staff four, none is required in the transcription of them. From an opposing point of view, the copyist puts no flats there because none is needed when the *b* is in the melodic position it holds at the end of staff three and in staff four. In each case the *b* is at an apex of a melodic contour, approached by step from below and subsiding to a lower pitch. There was an oft-quoted dictum,

> *Una nota supra la,*
> *Semper est canendum fa.* *

So the *b's* would have been flatted anyway, whether there was a flat in the manuscript or not.

But this argument is weakened by the fact that *b* is the apex in each of the two places where the source does include them. Why are they included there if none is required for proper rendition? The answer is that they are included there to avoid ambiguity, and having been used twice, are sufficient to stand throughout. The argument can go on and on. As yet scholars seldom are willing to accept any general rule that does not allow full consideration of each individual instance on its own merits. The neophyte in editing medieval music would be wise to follow a similar course, considering every possible rendition and marshalling every argument he can devise for each example.

It is entirely possible that during the middle ages all five of the versions were used. The performer should try them all. He should be warned, however, that what may sound strange at first hearing has a way of becoming increasingly attractive as one becomes accustomed to it.

In troubadour music, however, the most puzzling and controversial notational problem has to do with duration, not pitch. At best, troubadour music is ambiguous in this regard, and much controversy, some of it heated, has accompanied the attempt to interpret its temporal patterns. Of *Kalenda maia* alone, more than fifteen modern editions have been published over the last century, all of which differ from one another in greater or lesser degree,[4] especially with respect to the rhythmic values. Why did copyists choose an ambiguous system when they copied the repertory well after suitable temporal means had been devised? There is no conclusive answer, but it seems likely that it was copied so because an ambiguous system could serve for several different kinds of performance; since that was an age of considerable improvisation, a precise method was neither needed nor desired. In its present form the piece could have served for a performance by one person singing alone, or for a group of instruments, or for combinations of several different sizes. After all, monophonic notation does not require monophonic performance. After completing his own transcription, the reader is urged to attempt an arrangement of the piece with appropriate percussion and melody instruments—with dancing too, for the estampida was a dance.

Of the various methods of transcription the earliest was by means of black noteheads without

---

* A note above *la*,
 Is always sung *fa*.

any indication of the durations of pitches. This method has attracted later scholars as well; Curt Sachs and Hendrik Vanderwerf, for example, who reason that since the notation itself does not clearly fix durations, it should be left to the individual to determine them for himself, thus permitting the same flexibility to the modern scholar and performer that was the prerogative of his medieval counterpart. To do this, the modern person must familiarize himself thoroughly with the original language, the poem, the music, with all their interrelations, and then, from long acquaintance with the piece, he determines his own rhythmic patterns.

But if this method has arguments in its favor—and it is an excellent one for the study of the melody and its patterns—there are objections as well. The modern scholar-performer is at a disadvantage not shared by his medieval counterpart in that he has no frame of reference, or at best a very different one, from which to commence his study. Furthermore not everyone who could benefit from the study and performance of this repertory is also expert in the Provençal language. And even if he were he might benefit from some guidelines to stimulate his own efforts.

Another method of transcription is rendition into modal rhythm. Pioneers in this method were Pierre Aubry, Jean Beck, and Friedrich Ludwig. A little later the same principles were endorsed and extended by Friedrich Gennrich and Hans Spanke.[5] The reasoning here was that secular songs sometimes were used as *contrafacta* in polyphonic motets. Since motets used modal rhythmic patterns, the monophonic songs should also. To determine the rhythmic mode of a piece which had not been used in a polyphonic setting, one first determined the tonic accents of the words in the first line of the poem. After determining the prevailing rhythmic mode by that means, he applied it continuously to the remainder of the piece. Obviously this leads to a good deal of rigidity and often to the complete destruction of the form and rhythm of the poem itself.

Although transcription into strict rhythmic modes has been attacked repeatedly by both literary and musical scholars, many are reluctant to abandon the method entirely, for it does seem to apply to some songs in their entirety and to parts

of a great many others. Accordingly scholars such as Sesini, Anglès, Machabey, and Husmann[6] have suggested various modifications, most of which are derived from the various notational symbols. Their efforts have resulted in a loosening of the restrictions of a purely modal interpretation. It seems impossible to derive a clear interpretation of the meaning of the notation through consideration of the notation only, at least for a large part of the troubadour repertory. It is precisely this problem that led Vanderwerf to use noteheads only; no other system appears to yield fully consistent results.

The system proposed here lies about midway between a rigid rendition in rhythmic modes and the free rendition in black noteheads. It is based on poetic scansion and on analysis of the poem, considering each line and the functions of the individual words and syntactic groups that comprise each line. In this way it is possible to recognize the subtle changes that can arise within a line as the accent of an idea shifts within its changing context. There are six elements in a scansion and study of this kind: first, rhetorical groups; second, syntactic groups; third, breath groups; fourth, tonic accent of words; fifth, the idea accent arising from the context of each line in relation to all other lines; and sixth, the isochronous principle of a steadily recurring pulsation, translated in music as a beat, and the grouping of such beats into larger units so arranged as to incorporate the accents determined by the previous five elements of scansion.

The scansion of the first stanza served as the basis for the transcription appended to this study. At the outset it must be understood, however, that other scansions are possible. No unanimity exists or should exist in the matter of scansion or in the shades of understanding which each person brings to a piece of poetry. Flexibility must remain: this is *a* solution, not *the* solution. After studying the scansion and comparing it to the transcription, the reader should devise his own settings for the other stanzas of the poem.

None of the general problems encountered in *Kalenda maia* is unique, and the process of editing is a slow and labored one full of puzzles. But all one's efforts are richly rewarded by the experience of a delightful piece of music well worth knowing.

Kalenda maia

Raimbault de Vaqueiras
ed. by Gwynn S. McPeek

1. Ka - len - da mai - a, Ni fueills de fai - a, Ni chans d'au - zell ni flors de glai - a. Non es qe·m plai - a, Pros do - na gai - a, Tro q'un is - nell mes - sa - gier ai - a: Del vos - tre bell cors qe·m re - trai - a, Pla - zer no - vell q'a - mors m'a - trai - a: E jai - a, e·m trai - a vas vos, Don - na ve - rai - a. E chai - a, de plai - a ·l ge - los, Anz qe·m n'es-trai - a.

Kalénda máia
Ni fueills de fáia
Ni cháns d'auzéll ni flórs de gláia
Non és qe·m pláia
Pros dóna gáia
Tró q'un isnéll messágier aía;
Del vóstre bell córs, qe·m retráia,
Plazér novéll q'amórs m'atráia;
E jáia, e·m tráia vas vós,
Dónna veráia;
E cháia de pláia ·l gelós,
Anz qe·m n'estráia.

2. Ma bell' amia,
   Per Dieu non sia
   Qe ja·l gelos de mon dan ria,
   Qe car vendria
   Sa gelozia,
   Si aitals dos amantz partia;

   Q'ieu ja joios mais non seria,
   Ni jois ses vos pro no·m tenria;
   Tal via faria q'oms ja
   Mais no·m veiria;
   Cell dia morria, donna pros,
   Q'ie·us perdria.

3. Con er perduda
   Ni m'er renduda
   Donna, s'enanz non l'ai aguda?
   Qe drutz ne druda
   Non es per cuda;
   Mas qant amantz en drut si muda,
   L'onors es granz qe·l n'es creguda,
   E·l bels semblanz fai far tal bruda;
   Qe nuda tenguda no·us ai,
   Ni d'als vencuda;
   Volguda, cresuda vos ai,
   Ses autr' ajuda.

4. Tart m'esjauzira,
   Pos ja·m partira,
   Bells Cavalhiers, de vos ab ira,
   Q'ailhors no·s vira
   Mos cors, ni·m tira
   Mos deziriers, q'als non dezira;
   Q'a lauzengiers sai q'abellira,
   Donna, q'estiers non lur garira:
   Tals vira, sentira mos danz,
   Qi·lls vos grazira,
   Qe·us mira, cossira cuidanz,
   Don cors sospira.

5. Tant gent comensa,
   Part totas gensa,
   Na Beatritz, e pren creissensa
   Vostra valensa;
   Per ma credensa
   De pretz garnitz vostra tenensa
   E de bels ditz, senes failhensa;
   De faitz grazitz tenetz semensa;
   Siensa, sufrensa avetz
   E coneissensa;
   Valensa ses tensa vistetz
   Ab benvolensa.

6. Donna grazida,
   Qecs lauz' e crida
   Vostra valor q'es abellida,
   E qi·us oblida,
   Pauc li val vida,
   Per q'ie·us azor, donn' eissernida;
   Qar per gençor vos ai chauzida
   E per meilhor, de prez complida,
   Blandida, servida genses

Q'Erecs Enida.
Bastida, finida, n'Engles,
Ai l'estampida.

TRANSLATION

1. Neither May Day nor beech-tree leaf, nor song of bird nor gladiola flower can please me, noble and gay lady, until from your fair person there comes to me a fast messenger telling me of some fresh delight that love and joy bring me, and I repair to you, true-hearted lady, and the jealous one falls stricken, before I leave there.

2. My fair beloved, I pray God that the jealous one may never rejoice at my hurt, for he would sell his jealousy dearly if two such lovers were separated; never more would I be joyful, nor without you would joy be any good to me. I would take that path whereby no one ever would see me again; fine lady, the day I lost you, I should die.

3. How shall I lose a lady or regain her if first I have not possessed her? No man or woman becomes a lover by thought alone. But when the wooer becomes a lover, the honour which has come to him thereby is great, such is the fame produced by a kind glance. Yet I have not held you naked nor won aught else from you. I have desired you and put my faith in you without any reward.

4. Enjoyment would hardly come to me, fair knight, if I should depart from you in sorrow, for nowhere else does my heart turn or my desire draw me, since I desire naught else. Lady, I know that the slanderers would be well pleased, for in no other way could their malady be cured. Such a one would see and feel my anguish who would be beholden to you for it, as he contemplates you and meditates on you in his presumption, for which I sigh in my heart.

5. Lady Beatrice, your value blossoms and grows so exquisitely, and surpasses that of all other ladies. I believe you adorn your power with merit and pleasant words. You are the source of pleasing deeds. You have knowledge, patience and judgment, and beyond all disputing you clothe your worth in kindness.

6. Gracious lady, everyone praises and proclaims your worth, which gives such delight, and he who forgets you prizes his life only little, and so I worship you, noble lady; for I have chosen you as the most gracious and best of all, perfect in merit, and I have wooed you and served you better than did Eric his Enid. Lord *Engles* [that is, Boniface] the estampida I have composed is finished.

NOTES

1. The *Razo* and first stanza are in: Florence, Biblioteca Laurenziana, Plut. XLI, cod. 42, folio 44.

2. The manuscript sources are as follows: Paris, Bibliothèque Nationale, f. fr., 856, folio 125; Paris, Bibliothèque

Nationale, f. fr., 12474, folio 106; Paris Bibliothèque Nationale, f. fr. 22543 which has two copies, folio 62 with the music and folio 519 with text only; Barcelona, Biblioteca de Catalunya, ms. 146, folio 59. For a discussion of the manuscripts and the traditions they represent, see: Joseph Linskill, *The Poems of the Troubadour Raimbault de Vaqueiras*, The Hague, 1964, p. 184.

3. Most recently, Hendrik Vanderwerf, "The Chansons of the Trouvères: A Study in Rhythmic and Melodic Analysis," dissertation, Columbia University, 1964.

4. Among the most accessible editions are: Davison and Apel, *Historical Anthology of Music*, vol. I, p. 16, no. 18d; Arnold Schering, *Geschichte der Musik in Beispielen*, p. 6, no. 11. Interesting comparisons also may be made among the following: Restori in *Rivista musicale italiana* III (1896), p. 236; Riemann, *Handbuch der Musikgeschichte* (1905), I, p. 234; Aubry, *Trouvères et Troubadours* (1909), p. 56; Adler, *Handbuch der Musikgeschichte* (1924), I, p. 159 (transcription by Ludwig); Gennrich, *Troubadours, Trouvères, Minne- und Meistergesang* (1960), pp. 16; 68 (very like two other editions by the same editor: *Musikalische Nachlass der Troubadours* [1958], III, p. 100; *Formenlehre des Mittelalterlichen Liedes* [1932], p. 164); and Sesini in *Primordi della lirica d'arte in Italia*, ed. by V. DeBartholomaeis (1943), p. 27.

5. Aubry's ideas are expressed in *La Rhythmique musicale des troubadours et des trouvères* (1907) and in *Trouvères et troubadours* (1909), where he states his conclusions on pp. 191-192. Beck's ideas are found in *Les Chansonniers des troubadours et des trouvères*, vol. II: *Chansonnier Cangé, notes et commentaires*, introduction, especially pp. 48-71. Ludwig's ideas are summarized in the reference given in footnote 4 above. Gennrich's ideas are in the references in footnote 4 also. Spanke's views are expressed in his review of Beck's edition of the Cangé manuscript in *Zeitschrift für französische Sprache und Literatur*, LII (1929), 165ff.

6. For Sesini's views, in addition to the reference in footnote 4, see: "Le melodie troubadoriche nel Canzoniere provenzale della Biblioteca Ambrosiana (R. 71 Sup.)" in *Studi Medievali*, XVII (1939), 1-101. For Anglès's views see: *La Musica de las Cantigas de Santa Maria del Rey Alfonso el Sabio* (1943-1964); and "Rhythm in Medieval Lyric Monody," in *Report of the Eighth Congress of the International Musicological Society*, New York, 1961, pp. 3-11. For Machabey's views see: "Problèmes de notation musicale . . ." in *Mélanges de linguistique et de littérature romanes à la mémoire d'István Frank*, (1957), pp. 361-387; and his *Notations non modales des XIIᵉ et XIIIᵉ siècles* (1957-1958). Husmann's views are expressed specifically toward *Kalenda maia* in *Archiv für Musikwissenschaft*, X (1953), pp. 270-281.

2

A Comparison of Two Manuscripts:
Fole acoustumance (c. 1250)

HANS TISCHLER

INDIANA UNIVERSITY

The Montpellier Codex (Fac. de Méd. H.196) is one of the great monuments of early polyphony, indeed the central monument of mid-thirteenth-century art music as practiced by the connoisseur. It was truly a great event when Mme Yvonne Rokseth, just before World War II, published it in facsimile and two volumes of transcription, and then added a volume of analysis to her magnificent edition: *Polyphonies du XIIIe siècle* (1936-39). Ever since, this publication has held an outstanding place among the achievements of musical scholarship and fine music publishing, and has been looked upon as the greatest single source of information about the music of the century of St. Louis.

But a third of a century has passed since Mme Rokseth's work, and vast knowledge has been accumulated during that span of time. It stands to reason that a critical reappraisal of Rokseth's edition is called for and that new knowledge may unravel many knotty problems which Mme Rokseth solved with only partial success. As beautifully written as the codex is, it contains a fair share of human errors, omissions, and misreadings, to which the modern editor and printer have added a few of their own. Nearly every work in the two volumes

Two sources for the two-part motet "Fole acoustumance": (left) folios 85-86v of the Montpellier Codex—Faculté de Médecine H 196; (right) folios 218-218a of Wolfenbüttel Ms. 1206.

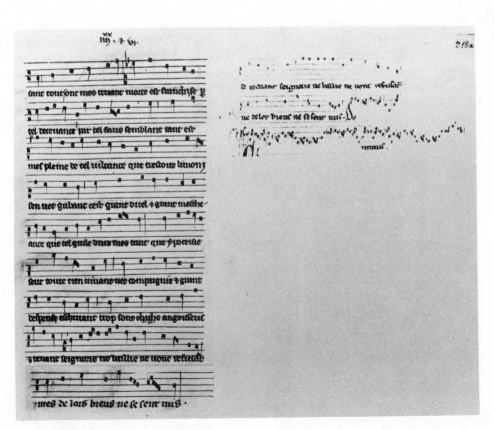

of transcriptions does, in fact, need some revision, many of them minor, but others of major proportion. These concern lacunae, accidentals, barring, note values, rhythm, the coordination of voices, pitches, the texts, their versification, rests, cadences, the reading of certain ornaments, and other features.

We have chosen a particularly interesting example which must be entirely recast from the form in which it appears in Rokseth's transcription to become viable as a piece of music. It is the last motet in the third fascicle (III,50), which in the codex is written without its tenor, as if it were a monophonic work. In a footnote Mme Rokseth shows her awareness of the fact that the tenor is merely omitted here. She also signifies her awareness of the existence of this piece in two other manuscripts, namely, W2 (Wolfenbüttel 1206) and MuA (Munich, gallo-rom.42 + Paris, Bibl.nat. Vma.1446), the latter known to her at the time only in an incomplete form, lacking the end of the motetus and the entire tenor. But the tenor is contained in W2, and a fourth manuscript, F (Florence, Bibl. Med. Laur. Pl.29,1), contains the entire music as well, although it is set to a Latin text and therefore not considered by Mme Rokseth. Strangely, although Mme Rokseth notes variants that occur in W2 and MuA, she has not gone to the trouble of transcribing the motet from the complete versions, and, therefore, since certain note and rest symbols may be read in several rhythmic ways, she arrives at a transcription that is totally wrong and, what is more, unmusical.

Two passages in the transcription below can serve as illustrations: measures 1-10 and 30-33. It will be immediately seen how Rokseth's barring of the first passage runs counter to the musical sense; moreover, the fine, song-like balance of 4+4+2 measures is completely destroyed in her rendition, which replaces it by 3+3½+1½. Contributing factors to this wrong rendition are the ambiguities of certain note symbols which shall be discussed below. But a simple transcription of the versions in W2 and/or F would have revealed which resolutions were to be chosen. Similarly, a significantly better reading of verse 3 could have been established in this way. —In the second passage we again see what havoc results from Rokseth's failure to draw on the other versions. Here a simple phrase of $\frac{a\ a1\ a2\ b}{1+1\ -\ 1+1}$ is completely ruined by making it extend over seven measures: 2+2+2+1. Here the factor contributing to the misinterpretation is a deviant notation which, however, occurs in several other pieces in the manuscript as well as in other sources. Again reference to the remaining versions would have clarified the situation.

In Rokseth's version this particularly well-wrought, song-like piece suffers further, as it is forced to go through six changes and reestablishments of the basic meter, has its melody falsified by the lack of the $B^{\flat}$ key signature that it should have throughout, and is faulty in the final cadence. The musical charm of this almost classical piece strangely contrasts with the biting moral criticism of both its texts, which offer a rare instance of a text replacement, a *contrafactum*, that is a real translation of the original text. Above the repeated tenor melody of 40+40+4 measures, the motetus, as the texted duplum is called, presents numerous parallel phrase arrangements as follows:

$$a\ a^1\ b \qquad c\ c^1\ b_1 \qquad d\ x\ d^1\ b_1{}^1 \qquad e \qquad e^1\ b_1{}^2$$
$$E\ E_1 E_2\ X$$
$$4-4+2 \qquad 4-4-2 \quad : \quad 2+2-2+3 \qquad 1+1+1+1-4-3 \quad //$$

$$f\ b_1{}^3\ f_1{}^1 \qquad g \qquad x \qquad g^1 \qquad h\ h_1{}^1\ h_1{}^1\ f_2{}^2\ h^2\ h_2{}^2 \quad f_2{}^3\ i\ y^1$$
$$G\ G_1\ G_2{}^1$$
$$2+4\ -2-\ 1+1+2-2- \qquad 2+2\ :\ 2+2-2+3-3-3\ -3-4-4$$

We may now proceed to a closer examination of the notation, and by juxtaposing the facsimiles from W2 and Mo we can contrast the main features of what are called square notation and mensural notation.

The former was created to serve the syllabic melodies of the motets. Its direct antecedent was the modal notation of the organa (itself derived from the Gregorian neumes) which indicated the rhythm of melismatic lines by means of series of ligatures, i.e., note groups (see next paragraph).

A series of such ligatures of 3, 2, and 2 notes

would mean [♩♩ ♪♪ ♪♪ ♪♩ ♪♩ ♪♩] ; a series of groups of 4, 3, and 3 notes would mean [♩ ♩. ♪♩ ♩ ♩. ♪♪♩ ♩ ♩. ♪♪♩ ♩ ♩.] , and so on. Once these ligatures were dissolved for the new purpose of serving texts, their rhythmic meaning vanished; the individual notes lack differentiation and are open to different interpretations. These interpretations depend on implications known to the performer from tradition and from the scant clues of the text rhythm. Only here and there attempts are made to give some indication by note shapes, e.g., by lengthening noteheads as at the end of the 4th brace in W2. But these are not consistently carried out. The few ligatures, whether written in square notes or diamond-shaped ones ("currentes"), are ornaments; like the single notes, they are open to various interpretations, which depend entirely on the place of the particular note or figure within the series of modal beats. The same is true of the lines that serve as rests (and also as mere commas). The only other help, often also (as here) ambiguous, comes from the modally written tenor, to which the upper part (or parts) must correspond.

All this changes in Mo. Here the *longa* (with a stem descending at the right of the notehead) and the *brevis* (simple square note) are carefully differentiated. Similarly the ligatures have different forms: some carry an ascending stem at the start, indicating that the two (sometimes also three or four) notes that follow are to be read as *semibreves* (e.g., at the end of the 2nd staff of the second page, in the middle of the 2nd staff on the third page, and in the last line); others indicate by their shapes that all the constituent notes are *breves* (e.g., the ligatures in lines 6-8 on the third page:

◗◣ , ◣ , ◪); yet others may include *longae*, but none of these occur in this particular piece (e.g.,

◼ and ◼◻ = ♪♩ and ♪♪). An irregularity we have already mentioned above in connection with the passage measures 30-33 occurs first in staves 2-4 of the second page. The series *longa—brevis—brevis—longa* normally indicates the third

mode: | ♩. ♪♪ | ♩. ; that this interpretation is wrong here is evident from our transcription. The habit of so notating a series of consecutive *breves* occurs elsewhere also, as already noted.

Like the notes, the rests are differentiated in mensural notation. See, for example, the short bar in the first line on the second page, signifying a *brevis* rest, and the long bar in the next line that occupies the value of a *longa*. However, the scribe was obviously uncertain about his rests on the first page, all of which should have been written as long bars, as also on the third page. The result of accepting these errors at face value affected the passage measures 1-10 discussed above, where Mme

Rokseth transcribes as ♩ 𝄿 what should be

rendered as ♩. 𝄾. . Note that the scribe of W2 also was human and misplaced several notes and words; he even omitted two entire passages, namely, measures 7-8 and 74-76. Another ambiguity that led to misinterpretations in the passage

measures 1-10 is that of the figure ◼ ◤◤ , which

may be read as either ♩ ♬ ³ or ♩. ♬ .

Otherwise the first mode (♩ ♪♪ ♪) is easily seen to prevail throughout in the alternation of *longae* and *breves*.

Fole acoustumance

Anonymous (13th century)
ed. by Hans Tischler

23. que l'on ne l'en voit bla-smant. 24. Chas-cun le va re - dou - tant, 25. n'il n'est mi - e

26. grant fo - li - e, 27. car li plus riche et li plus pois - sant

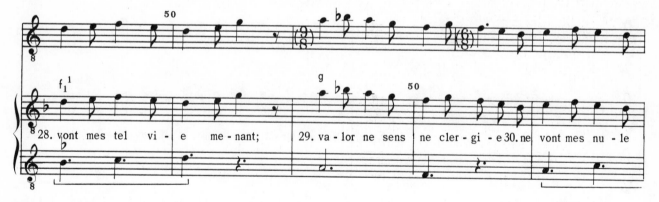

28. vont mes tel vi - e me - nant; 29. va - lor ne sens ne cler - gi - e 30. ne vont mes nu - le

rien pri - sant; 31. tout ont mes tru - ant. 32. Morte est Fran-ce 33. par tel de - ce - vance 34. et

45. ne bail-li - e 46. ne vont re - fu - sant, 47. mais de leur biens ne se

sent nus.

3

Lyonel Power's *Sanctus* (ca. 1410)

JOHN REEVES WHITE
HUNTER COLLEGE

This heavenly beautiful "C-major" Sanctus, composed around the first quarter of the fifteenth century, was first performed by the New York Pro Musica at the Cloisters on December 18, 1969, in memory of the poet, William Earle Nettles. On that occasion it was sung by three male singers—countertenor, tenor, and bass—with tenor viol, bass viol, and organ. It lends itself to a variety of ways of performance, however, some of which approach more closely the usual cathedral practice of Lyonel Power's early fifteenth-century England. Almost nothing is known of Power's life except for the report that he spent some time at Canterbury Cathedral and died at Winchester on June 5, 1445.

The unique copy of this work appears on f. 95v-96 of the Old Hall Manuscript, which preserves the majority of Power's compositions. These tower over the rest of the collection by their harmonic innovations, their expressive use of dissonance, their daring sumptuousness of vocal scoring, and simply their beauty. They seem to look fully a century ahead of Dunstable and Dufay. Several of them, as does this Sanctus, end on a full triad with the third present to the end (not common until a hundred years later), one bold sign of the remarkably original and beautiful things they contain. I have found their retrieval for modern audiences mandatory, despite the many thorny performance problems they raise. Their solution requires courage and even a measure of creativity, as we shall see.

The Old Hall Manuscript is believed by numerous scholars, including Frank Ll. Harrison and Andrew Hughes, to be a repertoire collected prior to 1413 mainly for St. George's Chapel, Windsor, on the basis of its contents and the provenance of its composers, including a "Roy Henry." Its subsequent history is unknown until 1813 when it was bought at auction for two guineas by John Stafford Smith, antiquarian-musician (in fact, the author of the tune of "The Star-Spangled Banner"). In 1893 his heirs presented the priceless collection to St. Edmund's College, Old Hall, near Ware in Hertfordshire, now its permanent home. But alas, by that time some vandal had excised nineteen of its illuminated initials, including the "S" of our Sanctus and likewise the initial of the following piece on f. 96v., robbing us probably forever of two passages in the voice part I call Tenor I: measures 15-18 and measures 29-33. Unfortunately, they cannot be reconstructed but must be freshly composed in the spirit of their surroundings and from acquaintance with other works of Power similar in texture and style. My version differs from that of A. Ramsbotham who first edited the Old Hall Manuscript for the Plainsong and Medieval Music Society (Vol. III, [1938], pp. 70-75) and that of Andrew Hughes who has prepared a new edition with Margaret Brent for the American Institute of Musicology. Mr. Hughes kindly shared his edition of the Sanctus with me before publication, as well as the information that three notes of the Tenor II, measures 59-60, invisible in the photograph, are to be found under the patched initial on f. 95v, a crude attempt to repair the vandalism. His edition also makes clear the numerous passages of red coloration, which cannot be seen in the black-and-white facsimile, nor were they recorded by Ramsbotham. In this score they are marked by broken brackets (⌐ ⌐) and ligatures by full brackets (▭).

Power's layout of voices and text is very common in early fifteenth-century music: two parts for high tenor voices supplied with text (which might be called Triplex I on f. 95v and Triplex II on f. 96) and two textless voices in baritone and bass range which are labeled Tenor

Lyonel Power, *Sanctus*, Old Hall Manuscript, folio 95v-96. Courtesy of St. Edmund's College, Ware, Hertfordshire.

and Contratenor by the scribe. Power's Tenor has no cantus firmus—rather it is the Triplex I which intones first the incipit of the Gregorian Sanctus IV (*Liber Usualis*, p. 27, for Double Feasts of the First Class) and continues to spin out an inventive paraphrase of this melody, referring always to the Gregorian motives at the outset of each new phrase of the text. These references would be easily recognized by those who had the Gregorian melody by heart.

My first decision was to assign the trailing, more agile Triplex II of the Sanctus and Osanna, with its somewhat higher tessitura, to a modern countertenor singer (in our score designated Tenor I), while delegating to him the intonation and very agile Triplex I of the Benedictus. A modern tenor singer of slightly greater weight (designated Tenor II) thus bears in the main the responsibility for the Gregorian paraphrase and the slower moving of the two high voices.

Problems remain for the parts Power designated Tenor and Contratenor, written largely in ligatures. The options are few: (1) several bass and baritone singers vocalizing on the long phrases and staggering their breathing; (2) an organ or a "payre of organs" playing these constantly crossing lower voices which would be sensible only for two players reading from the same part-book; (3) an organist playing from a written-out score underlining some or all of the parts, and of course no such thing survives from that period; (4) singers with or without sustaining instruments underlaying the familiar Sanctus text at sight and ignoring the relation between ligatures and syllable-distribution; (5) the participation of other instruments.

Frank Ll. Harrison devotes some pages of his *Music in Medieval Britain* (London, 1958) to the problems of performance, especially pages 202-219, "The Medieval Organ" and "The Ritual Use of the Organ." While he finds only one citation of "other instruments," shawms and bells for a Te Deum at St. Alban's before 1527, in that year Cardinal Wolsey heard a Te Deum at St. Paul's "solemnlie sungen with the King's trumpets and shalmes as well Inglishmen as Venetians" (—King Henry's Italian viols?). His investigations then strongly support the performance of voices alone or with organ(s) as the normal way, while allowing the rare appearance of other melodic instruments such as shawms (bordones), bells, and perhaps vielles.

Certain practical questions emerge. What was the role of a bass singer in the elaborate choirs of the English cathedrals—only to vocalize, never to sing the sacred text? Were the most elaborate and beautiful compositions of Old Hall, such as Power's five-voice Gloria (Vol. I, pp. 60-64, where suddenly

and inexplicably the word "Amen" appears in the last nine measures of the two lowest voices) designed exclusively for high tenors and bunched-together organ lines? These practical considerations led us to dare to underlay the Sanctus text to our present Contratenor part (Bass II), ignoring the ligatures as a singer would do if he ever *did* sing the familiar words. The magnificent outburst of this voice at the beginning of the last Osanna, one of the marvelous moments of this altogether exceptional composition, seems reason enough to demand that it be "sung to words." The same "sight-singing" of text might be applied to Power's Tenor, though I did not in this edition.

The most modern and controversial aspect of the present transcription is the distribution of text for the two tenors, permitting the repetition of phrases and ignoring much of the scribe's underlay. His is often haphazard, frequently disregarding the possible relation of the text to the melodic phrase and the cadential structure (e.g., measures 5-7 of Triplex I which the scribe ends on "Sanc-" and measures 26-33 where the word "gloria" is twice broken by rests). Since this unique manuscript copy implies in no way the sanction of the composer, we choose to try to parallel his musical intensity with a clarity of verbal expression, giving important words to high points of phrases, allowing the listener an intelligible flow of the text. There is nothing definitive in the present version. In performance other ways may be found, indeed should be sought out, as I believe the best singers would have done in fifteenth-century cathedrals.

In conclusion, a summary of various ways this work might be performed:

1. A "chamber version" with solo voices and instruments either early or modern—bass clarinet and bassoon would serve beautifully, while the New York Pro Musica employed viols and small positive organ.

2. A fully choral performance, with the lower pair of voices vocalizing or realizing the text.

3. Solo tenors gently supported by a choir of baritones and basses.

4. Various combinations of voices and organ, the latter providing a polyphonic part or an accompaniment, for which this edition supplies a short score.

The tempo cannot be too slow—the singers' breathing will help to regulate this at ca. $\goodbreak$ = 76-92. The most important advice is that each singer realize the curve and intensity of his own part. The composer has done the rest.

SANCTUS

Lyonel Power
ed. by John Reeves White

21

4

An Editorial Problem in a Mass
by Heinrich Isaac (c. 1450-1517):
Sanctus and *Benedictus* from
Missa Misericordias Domini

GUSTAVE REESE

NEW YORK UNIVERSITY

The rhythm of Renaissance music presents at the same time one of its main delights and one of its most difficult challenges. The actual sound, fortunately, produces the delight. The problems, as is all too well known, become thorny if one tries to find precise parallels for certain aspects of that rhythm in written form. The rhythm is not always at odds with normal notation, but the two do prove incompatible with disturbing frequency.

Among the fifteenth-century composers who have left us particularly choice examples of Renaissance rhythms is Heinrich Isaac, whose lofty position among composers of the Josquin generation Professor Cuyler has done so much to clarify. The rhythmic felicities of his *Hélas que devera mon cuer* and *Et qui la dira* are well known. Those in the Benedictus of his four-part *Missa Misericordias Domini* are not. The Mass, printed in 1506 in Ottaviano Petrucci's *Misse henrici Izac*, has never been published complete in a modern edition. A dozen measures, printed as a musical illustration in the present author's *Music in the Renaissance*, appear to be the only portion of the work available in modern score. (They begin at measure 55, beat 3, in the differently barred edition printed herewith.) Two of the four voices in those dozen measures contain nonsynchronizing five-beat sequences against the prevailing binary meter of the other two parts. While, in the Sanctus through *Osanna I*, the rhythm is fairly straightforward, it is rather intricate throughout the Benedictus. The purpose of this contribution is to present the Sanctus-Benedictus complete and to suggest a way in which editorial technique might make the rhythmic character of the piece immediately and easily evident to the eye.

The proposed procedure leans heavily on the methods of Otto Gombosi, though it is perhaps a bit simpler. Prior to his death in 1955, Gombosi's methods enjoyed a certain vogue, at least in scholarly circles, but recently they have been somewhat under a cloud. However, they have not become so obscure as to require more than a general description in these comments. The main point is that bars are inserted, at regular or irregular time intervals, in accord with what is believed to be the rhythmic sense of the music.

Gombosi's own major publication applying his distinctive procedures is his edition of the manuscript lutebook, dating from 1517, *Compositione di Meser Vincenzo Capirola* (Neuilly-sur-Seine: Société de musique d'autrefois, 1955). Here solid bar lines run sometimes through a single staff, sometimes through both staves, with differing significance; dotted bar lines, having their own special meaning, also at times run through a single staff. Because the music is for a solo instrumentalist, conflicting accentuation in different musical lines does not play the important role that it does in Renaissance ensemble music, whether for voices or for instruments, and, where solid bars do not run through the two staves, they are nevertheless vertically aligned. However, Gombosi also worked out ways of indicating nonsimultaneous accentuation in ensemble music,[1] the kind of accentuation with which we shall be mainly concerned in discussing our Isaac example.

The Gombosi type of barring has been criticized on several grounds. One is that the rhythmic sense of the music may be susceptible of interpretation in more than one way and that the editor's interpretation should not be imposed upon the user. This is certainly a correct view. However, methods have been found that are clear and simple enough to distinguish editorial accidentals in the application of *musica ficta* from accidentals in the

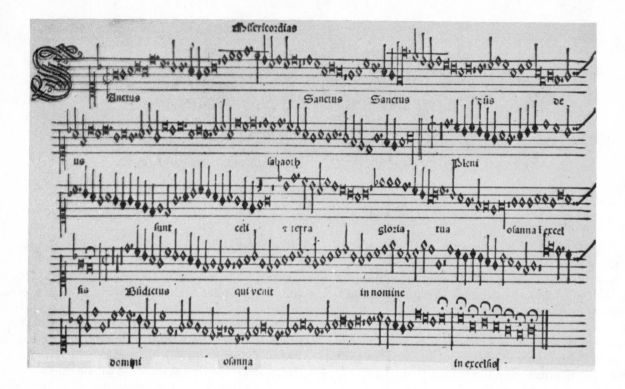

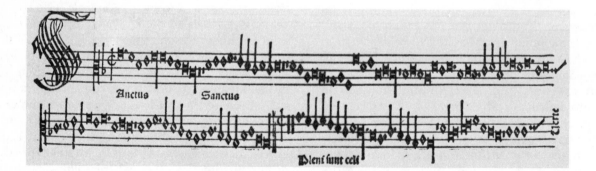

The four parts of Isaac's *Missa Misericordias Domini* from Petrucci's *Misse henrici Izac*, 1506.

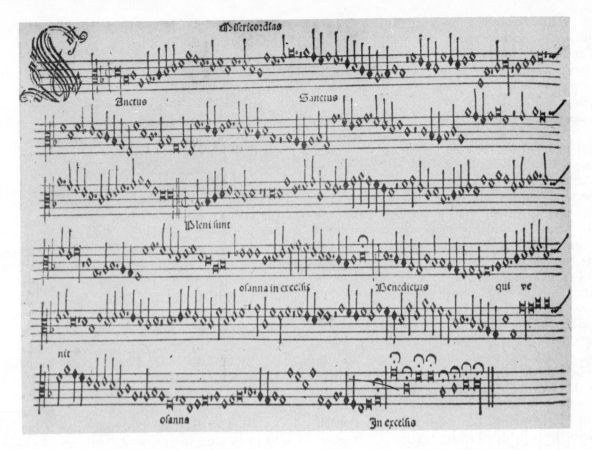

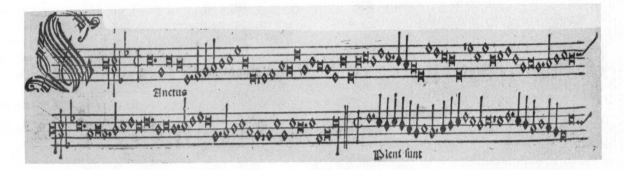

sources. It should be possible to convey an editor's ideas concerning the rhythm as merely his suggestions and at the same time to distinguish his barring from such barring as results when one indicates measure-lengths according to the mensuration signature.

Another objection to the Gombosi methods is that the appearance of the printed page becomes too complicated for the comfort of the performer. It is held that sufficiently musical performers can and do accentuate in the right places even if bars appear at regular intervals—whether these run through the staves or merely through the space between them (producing what the Germans call the *Mensurstrich*). This is admittedly a strong argument, but it applies mainly to performers already familiar with the flexibility of Renaissance rhythm.

Still another objection is that, where the accentuation does not change in all parts simultaneously, bars (of whatever nature) spaced irregularly not only with regard to the rhythm, but also in relation to the different parts, present excessive difficulties in conducting. This objection seems not to be well-founded, since the problems disappear if the conductor simply beats the *tactus*. Where all the parts change their accentuation at the same time—no matter how irregularly—no serious problems should result for musicians of a period such as ours, in which Stravinsky is regarded virtually as a classic.

Another hurdle may arise from the difficulty of making references, in a critical apparatus, to specific measures, if the measures do not consistently begin and end at the same places in all parts. This can readily be overcome by indicating the basic mensuration in some way that will not excessively clutter up the page and by having references in the apparatus apply to that mensuration.

Notwithstanding all the possible objections, barring according to the editor's sense of the rhythm does seem to have its place. We have differing readings of the standard symphonies according to the various major conductors. Why not differing readings of Renaissance compositions according to various conductors—and musicologists? As we have signified above, we feel that it is possible to convey an individual reading graphically without misleading the user into accepting it as something clearly indicated by the original notation. We have tried, in our example, to show what we believe the sense of the rhythm to be (espe-

cially important in the Benedictus) and also what the original mensuration is, without overloading the page.

Even if printed scholarly editions should probably remain free of one man's subjective ideas, a "practical" edition might incorporate them if that can be done simply enough not to render the edition "impractical." At the very least, there might be more preparation of flexibly barred, rhythmically analytical *handwritten* scores. (After all, it is not customary to print a symphony according to the readings of individual conductors.) Their function could be twofold. The student who prepares such a score himself inevitably analyzes passages that are rhythmically complex in a manner that makes him grasp their minute details intellectually. The preparation of such a score can also be a powerful aid to performers even before they begin to rehearse. This is especially true of performers who are not well acquainted with Renaissance rhythms.[2]

In the light of the foregoing, the Isaac Sanctus is herewith presented in a way that it is hoped will make the rhythmic refinements immediately evident to the eye without the page becoming excessively cluttered. The procedure involves simply (1) a consistent use of *Mensurstriche* throughout to indicate the mensuration and the macrorhythm; (2) solid bars from the top to the bottom of a staff where the microrhythm supersedes the macrorhythm in any one part; and (3) dotted bars from the top to the bottom of a staff to show the distribution of the subdivisions of the measures indicated by the solid bars, where more than one possibility exists (e.g., to show that five beats are distributed 2+3, not 3+2, or that eight beats are distributed 3+3+2).

NOTES

1. See, for example, *Journal of the American Musicological Society* I (1948), 52. Earlier attempts at flexible barring were made by Hugo Leichtentritt, e.g., in Vol. I of the Peters Edition (No. 3232a) of Monteverdi, *Madrigale* (n.d.). See also Leichtentritt, "On Editing Netherland Music," *The Musical Mercury* II (1935), 5-11.

2. Professor Lowinsky, who disapproves of irregular barring in printed editions would probably concede its justifiability in scores prepared for rhythmic analysis, whether for stylistic study or for study prior to performance. See Edward Lowinsky, "Early Scores in Manuscript," *Journal of the American Musicological Society* XIII (1960), 157f.

Missa Misericordias Domini:
Sanctus and *Benedictus*

Heinrich Isaac
ed. by Gustave Reese

37

1) B♮ in source.

2) Separate notes in the source.
3) The G is missing in the source.

5

A German Organ Tablature:
Dies est laetitiae (c. 1500)

THOMAS WARBURTON
UNIVERSITY OF NORTH CAROLINA AT CHAPEL HILL

Fridolin Sicher included three different Christmas songs in his organ tablature (Saint Gall, Stiftsbibliothek, Codex 530). He copied six settings of *Resonet in laudibus*, one of which he had composed, one setting of *In dulci jubilo*,[1] and a setting of *Dies est laetitiae* (fol. 9v). The last composition named is one of the few works in the manuscript that does not appear to be the transliteration of a vocal composition.

In the table of contents for his manuscript, Sicher made an entry under letter *D*, "Dies est leticie 9," the number to the right referring to the folio. Under the letter *M* is the entry "M Martini Vogelmaier 9." (Another complete composition, nowhere identified, occupies the entire fol. 9r. Sicher's folio numbers refer inconsistently either to verso or recto.) It is possible then that the brief Christmas composition was written by Vogelmaier, who was Johannes Buchner's predecessor at the Cathedral of Constance and Sicher's teacher in Constance in 1504.[2]

In organ tablatures of the early sixteenth century, a combination of letters and notes made it possible to show in a coordinated system music whose parts were usually separated either on different pages of a choirbook or in part books. The part highest in range is notated on a staff, and the remaining parts from highest to lowest indicated below the staff in letters. To the left of the staff, the lines for *c'*, the *g'* above, and the *d"* above that are marked by letters. At the end of some staves, Sicher placed the customary custos (w) to indicate the pitch at the beginning of the next line. In the lettered parts, the twelve notes of the octave, beginning with small *c*, are represented as follows:

The loops on *c*, *d*, *f*, and *g* indicate the inflections a half step upward. A dash above a letter indicates the octave above. Capital letters or a small curve (⌣) below a letter indicate the lower octave. The letter system, giving a different symbol for each key, is inherently more precise than staff notation. Whereas inflections were not always notated on the staves of sixteenth-century manuscripts and prints, the letters of the tablature could show the inflections exactly. German tablatures later in the century would adopt a system of letters for all parts.

Different ways in which inflections are notated reveal the disparity between staff and letters in tablature notation. While lettered parts show only upward inflections, notes on the staff can be affected by upward and downward inflections, both indicated by a tail extending below the notehead with a slash through it ( ). On the staff a *d* is never inflected, while Sicher used the letter *d* with a loop to represent an *e* flat. Similarly, *g* sharp is seen to represent *a* flat in the lettered parts. On the staff, a *b* flat is accomplished by an accidental sign, but *b* and *h* distinguish *b* flat and *b* natural in the lettered parts. The following table compares the two systems.

In the present composition, the notated *f* sharp of the bass line (measure 14) at the cadence for the

Dies est lastitiae by Martin Vogelmaier. Organ tablature of Fridolin Sicher (Saint Gall, Stiftsbibliothek, Codex 530), folio 9v.

reiteration of the opening phrase suggests a similar inflection in the first statement of the phrase (measure 6).

Rhythm is shown by a series of black note values. The largest value, a semibreve, is indicated by a dot above a letter or by a single diamond-shaped head on the staff. It is commonly represented by a half-note in transcription. The remaining values relate minim to quarter, semiminim to eighth, fusa to sixteenth, and semifusa to thirty-second. The tactus units, each a semibreve in length, are separated by a noticeable space. The definite visual groupings confirm the regular duple pulse of the music. (In his intabulation of *In dulci jubilo*,[3] in triple proportion, Sicher had notated the minim as a semiminim with an added upward stem and flag.) The irregular grouping of three minims (measure 31) reestablishes the regular pulse of the melody, whose last phrase had entered a "beat late" in the previous measure (measure 30).

In the four-part setting of *Dies est laetitiae*, the tenor line carries the melody, later to be the basis of the German chorale *Der Tag der ist so freudenreich*. Since Sicher's organ at Saint Gall had pedal stops, it would be appropriate to perform the composition with the tenor melody heard on a pedal reed. Furthermore, the digital complexities of such passages as measures 11-12, 17-19, and 26-28 would be greatly facilitated by playing the tenor line on the pedal keyboard.

NOTES

1. A facsimile of *In dulci jubilo* is given in Apel, *The Notation of Polyphonic Music* (Cambridge, 1961), p. 31.

2. *Fridolin Sichers Chronik*, ed. by Goetzinger, in Vol. 20 of *Mitteilungen zur vaterlaendischen Geschichte* (St. Gall, 1885), p. 35.

3. Apel, *loc. cit.*

Dies est laetitiae

Martin Vogelmaier (?)
ed. by Thomas Warburton

6

A Madrigal in Four Voices:
La mia doglia s'avanza (1613)
by Pomponio Nenna (c. 1550—c. 1618)

GLENN E. WATKINS
THE UNIVERSITY OF MICHIGAN

The preparation of an edition of *La mia doglia s'avanza* by Pomponio Nenna presents problems common to many Italian madrigals of the last two decades of the sixteenth century, particularly those of a chromatic character.

Accidentals. As a Neapolitan and associate of Carlo Gesualdo, it is no wonder that Nenna shares many features of that composer's style, and the question of accidentals in the present example suggests a solution in accord with principles which have evolved in the preparation of editions of his music. Characteristically, as with Gesualdo, sharps in the original are repeated before each pitch so affected, even in a series of repeated notes; a single flat, however, employed before a series of repeated notes is valid for all members of the series without a repetition of the sign until cancelled by a natural or sharp (alto, measure 25; basso, measure 26) or a rest. The suppression of redundant sharps (tenor, measures 4-5) or addition of implicit flats and natural signs (all voices, measures 21-25) according to these principles is implemented in the present edition in the interest of achieving a score which is not only modern in appearance but reliable in performance. Accidentals whose validity is conjectural, while absent here, would normally be placed above the note in question; to so locate accidental signs whose placement and validity are indisputable would falsify the intent of the original.

Clefs. Only modern clefs have been utilized, while the original clef indications are noted at the beginning of the piece, here SATB. In more unusual range combinations, the inclusion of original clef indications can be helpful in determining the vocal requirement at a glance.

Note Values. The range of note-values in the late sixteenth-century Mannerist repertoire normally precludes the reduction of note values. While it would be possible to halve values in the present example, this has not been done here, in the hope of facilitating a more ready comparison with other works of Nenna and his contemporaries. The note values, then, are original.

Metric Signs. There are only two in the original and they are both presented in the edition without change. C was the typical signature of the madrigal of the period in contradistinction to the use of ¢ for the motet. Implicit in this choice was a slightly slower tactus for C than ¢, reflecting the characteristic range of note values mentioned above. The momentary appearance of a 3, later cancelled by the return of C, is a relatively common feature of madrigals of the period. The problem inherent in such a change, of course, is one of tempo. While the direct proportional relationship inferable from such signs in music of the High Renaissance cannot be claimed, the equations $\textdownbow$ (C) = $\circ$ (3) at measure 16 and $\circ$ (3) = $\textdownbow$ (C) at measure 21 provide a reasonable and musical basis for performance. A three-to-one ratio ($\textdownbow$ = $\circ\cdot$) proves too fast, a three-to-two ratio ($\circ$ = $\circ\cdot$) too slow for the triple meter section.

Barring. A consistent use of even length measures of $\frac{4}{2}$ for the portions of the music in C and of $\frac{3}{2}$ for the portions in 3 has been maintained with the exception of measure 15. In light of the half-measure imposed at that point from such barring, a re-barring of measures 7-15 into measures of $\frac{4}{4}$ would not only be defensible but consistent to a degree with the fluctuating measure lengths of $\frac{6}{2}$, $\frac{4}{2}$, and $\frac{4}{4}$ found in Simone Molinaro's 1613 edition of the six volumes of Gesualdo's five-voice madrigals. The changes there, however, reflect less the vagaries of an editor than the actual disposition of the music, which is subjected to such a manner of barring only when the predominant note values of successive sections are dramatically dissimilar. This condition does not prevail in the Nenna example, however, and such a barring therefore has not been adopted.

Sources. Two editions of Nenna's *Primo libro à 4*, which date from 1613 and 1621, are known. A number of the madrigals contained therein, however, appeared earlier individually, and elsewhere I have submitted evidence to suggest that the entire set of four-voice madrigals may have been written as many as nine or ten years prior to the earliest surviving edition.[1] The final version of 1621 has served as the basis of the present edition.

Performance. The 1621 edition of the four-voice madrigals carries on its title page the following advertisement: *"Novamente ristampati, & con ogni diligenza corretti, Con l'Aggiunta del Basso Continuo Da Carlo Milanutio"* (newly reprinted and corrected, with the addition of a basso continuo by Carlo Milanutio). Milanuzzi's new addition is in reality only a figured *basso seguente* with trivial alterations and an occasional transposition of the part down a perfect fifth or fourth. Not being a product of the composer, it is omitted here.

NOTE

1. *Carlo Gesualdo, His Life and Music* (Oxford University Press, 1973).

TEXT

La mia doglia s'avanza
Quanto più la speranza
Ohimè, vien meno.

Il desio si rinfranca
Quant'ella manca,
E nel aspro martire
Il soverchio dolor non fa morire.

My pain deepens
the more that hope,
alas, fades.

Desire grows
the longer she is away,
and within the torn martyr
boundless sorrow does not bring death.

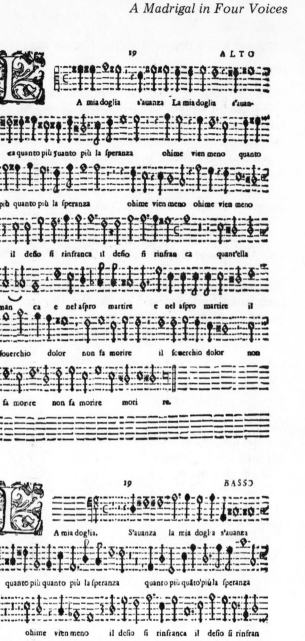

The four parts of the Madrigal *La mia doglia s'avanza* by Pomponio Nenna. From *Primo libro a 4.*

La mia doglia s'avanza

Pomponio Nenna
ed. by Glenn E. Watkins

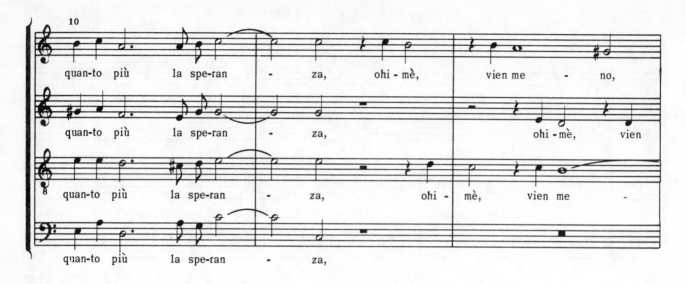

A Study of Notational and Performance Problems of an Early *Air de cour:*
Je voudrois bien, ô Cloris (1629) by Antoine Boësset (c. 1586-1643)

ALBERT COHEN

STATE UNIVERSITY OF NEW YORK—BUFFALO

Problems inherent in preparing a modern edition of an early *air de cour* are those that generally characterize the transcription of music originally intended to serve as a basis for improvised performance. Assuming that the editor can provide answers to the myriad questions of performance practice related to the source, how does he translate these into actual notational symbols so that the modern performer may be made aware of the practice that typified the original? How does he convey a feeling for the earlier style, or an understanding that the transcription being offered is but one result of choices made from the many available to the performer, and that other choices would have resulted in a different (though not less typical) composition?

The options available to performers of airs were numerous. The medium was flexible; only the treble tune, sung by a soloist, was immutable. The variety of different ways in which airs could be performed is clearly shown by the great diversity in format given to them in original sources (both printed and manuscript): they appear as one-part treble tunes, as two-part settings (the lower part being either a vocal line, or a one-line instrumental part, or a thorough-bass—figured or unfigured), as settings for 3-5 voices, and as songs to plucked-string (preferably lute) accompaniment. Indeed, concordances for a given air normally include sources having several such varying formats. The medium was easily adaptable to the exigencies of a given performance situation.

Airs are strophic works, usually supplied with many verses, and the performer had a certain degree of freedom in choosing those verses he wished to sing (after the first), and in deciding whether or not to take written (or unwritten) repeats. The purpose of repeats, of course, was to provide the soloist with an opportunity to embellish the vocal line, which characteristically was made increasingly more ornate upon each repetition. The manner of embellishment depended upon both the skill of the performer and the choice of medium. But it also was conditioned by historical period and locale, for preference in manner of ornamenting a vocal line continued to change throughout the time that the air had currency.

Writers of the time speak of the type of voice most suitable to the singing of airs—even and supple in quality, true in pitch, and moderate in dynamics. The singer was expected to phrase in accordance with the text, which had to be clearly enunciated. The end result was to charm the ear through a "sweetness" of sound ("la douceur françoise").

Generally speaking, wide variation in notational features is characteristic of the early air, since the manner of notating an *air de cour* often depended on the performance medium for which a given edition was originally intended. Versions set as part-songs are normally in part-books using, essentially, Renaissance notation. The two-part format (for two voices, or for solo voice and instrumental bass) is frequently in score. In settings for solo voice and lute, the tablature is arranged, line-by-line, immediately beneath the corresponding melody and text of the vocal part.

Bar lines, when found in an air, are ordinarily used irregularly as means of marking off phrases and of providing a visual aid for keeping the parts together; they rarely relate to meter signatures in a modern sense. Like much French vocal music of the time, airs are typified by frequent change of meter to accommodate changes in scansion of text. However, the exact relationship between pairs of consecutive metrical signs is not always clear in the

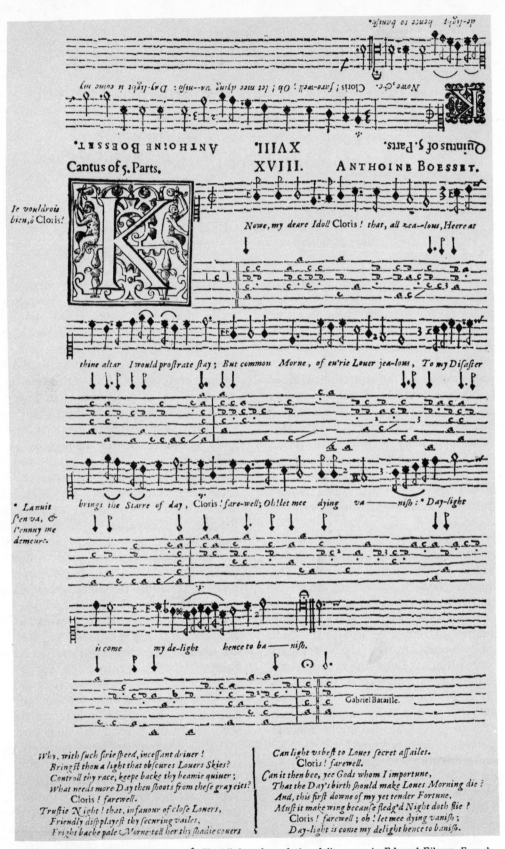

Antoine Boësset's "Je voudrois bien, ô Cloris" found on facing folio pages in Edward Filmer, *French Court-Ayres* (London: pr. by Wm. Stansby, 1629), No. XVIII. The item is reproduced by permission of *The Huntington Library,* San Marino, California.

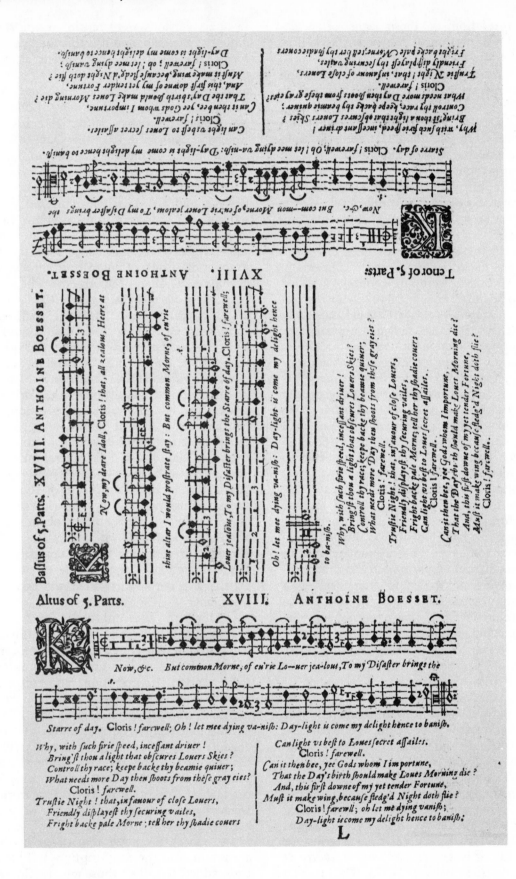

Altus of 5. Parts.   XVIII.   ANTHOINE BOESSET.

Now, &c.   But common Morne, of eu'rie Lo—uer jea-lous, To my Disaster brings the

Starre of day.   Cloris ! farewell; Oh ! let mee dying va-nish: Day-light is come my delight hence to banish.

Why, with such firie speed, incessant driuer !
  Bring'st thou a light that obscures Louers Skies?
  Controll thy race; keepe backe thy beamie quiuer;
  What needs more Day then shoots from these gray eies?
    Cloris ! farewell.
Trustie Night ! that, in fauour of close Louers,
  Friendly displayest thy securing vailes,
  Fright backe pale Morne ; tell her thy shadie couers

Can light vs best to Loues secret assailes.
    Cloris ! farewell.
Can it then bee, yee Gods whom I importune,
  That the Day's birth should make Loues Morning die ?
  And, this first downe of my yet tender Fortune,
  Must it make wing, because sledg'd Night doth flie ?
    Cloris ! farewll ; oh let me dying vanish ;
    Day-light is come my delight hence to banish;

L

source; interpretation of these signs often depended on the discretion of the singer, as well as on performance tradition.

Tempo is a particular problem when dealing with the early air, since it was governed more by an attitude (called "musique d'air") than by a scheme of more-or-less fixed rates of speed. Seventeenth-century sources note that the performer beats time almost to each note ("quasi à chaque note") of an air, regardless of time value, and that the singer should not be constrained by a rigid tempo; rather, he should have the liberty to dwell on whichever note (or notes) he wishes—notably when repeating sections or supplying embellishments.

Realization of thorough-bass lines raises yet other questions regarding interpretation, especially since these bass parts were not normally supplied with figures before about 1650. Also, where accompaniments are in tablature, there inevitably arises the matter of whether, in a modern transcription, to interpret them in polyphonic or homophonic texture. Studies of different versions of specific airs originating in varying formats has shown that accompanimental parts were generally intended to be chordal in nature, and often to do little more than supply the missing voices of a part-setting—although, most certainly, the performer of this instrumental part was expected to add musical interest.

Application of ornamentation is probably the single most difficult problem to resolve for the modern performer, since both the variety and quantity depend in large measure on the individual singer. Through reference to ornamented versions of airs that date from earlier periods, and particularly to manuals of the time that deal with embellishment practice, it is at least possible to suggest to the modern performer ways of applying ornamentation characteristic of the earlier practice.

Antoine Boësset's "Je voudrois bien, ô Cloris" serves as an illustration of notational problems representative of the *air de cour* at an early stage of development (that is, from before 1650-60, the early air being typically more free and less predictable in performance than the later air). The work was originally printed in at least three different formats: for voice and lute (*Airs de différents autheurs, mis en tablature de luth par Gabriel Bataille. Sixiesme livre*. Paris: P. Ballard, 1615); the treble tune by itself, with embellishments (*Airs de cour et de différents autheurs*. Paris: P. Ballard, 1615); and a five-part version for voices (Antoine Boësset. *Airs de cour à quatre et cinq parties*. Paris: P. Ballard, 1617). The lute and

five-part versions were reprinted in a source originating in England, and it is this English edition that forms the basis for the current study: *French Court-Aires . . . of foure and five Parts. Together with that of the lute . . . Collected, Translated, Published, by Ed[ward]. Filmer*. London: printed by William Stansby, 1629. Filmer's collection, which is dedicated "To the Queene" (*i.e.*, Henrietta Maria, youngest daughter of Henry IV of France and Marie de Médicis, who married Charles I of Great Britain in 1625), is limited to airs by Boësset and Guédron, all reprinted from French sources, but with texts translated into English. The work has historical significance; it demonstrates the influence of the early seventeenth-century French air (itself, affected by Italian style) on the development of the English air of the same period.

The collection is organized in such a manner as to make available alternate methods of performance. On facing folio pages, two different versions are given for each of the airs included in the edition: one for lute and treble voice, and the other for voices alone. The format of the lute and voice version differs little from the original French source, unlike the part-song version, which is rearranged so that it could be performed by a group of singers seated around a table, all reading from the same book. This general format, virtually unknown in France, is a typical one for the publication and performance of ayres and part-songs in England early in the seventeenth century, as is the English practice of providing a song with alternate possibilities of performance. Given this format, for example, the air could be sung by a single treble voice, or by treble and bass voices, or by the five parts—all with or without lute accompaniment.

Most of the notational and performance problems generally characteristic of the early *air de cour*, as discussed above, are present in Filmer's edition of Boësset's air, and they require resolution for a modern transcription. The editor must first decide whether to make available the alternate methods of performance given by Filmer, or to choose one from among them as the basis for an edition. This decision, in large part, will influence the nature of the modern reading. For present purposes, it was decided to retain the intent of the original as closely as possible. The work has been transcribed in open-score for voices and lute (or harpsichord with lute stop).

Changes of meter that occur in the original are retained in the transcription, but bar lines have been added to reflect those meters. Concerning the desirability of relating all the meters of an air to a common beat, Filmer states the following in his preface:

> Note that the usuall English measure of Songs (which is commonly by Sembriefs or Minoms) cannot be applyed to diverse of the French Aires. Where therefore you shall find an odde Crotchet in the Aire, measure the whole Aire by Crotchets; and, where an odde Minom, by Minoms.

Indeed, it is the crotchet (quarter-note) that is the "odde" note in the various meters of Boësset's air and, consequently, it is this note that serves as the beat in the present edition. The tempo designation is intended to serve only as a guide to the singer, who is to be permitted some latitude in varying the speed in performance, especially when embellishing his part.

Of the four verses given by Filmer, only the first, in English translation, is underlayed for all the parts in the source. Three additional verses, in English, are placed beneath each of the parts (except for the Quintus, there not being enough space to allow for the verses beneath this part); the French originals are appended to the rear of Filmer's collection.

In the current edition, the verses are given in both English and French (using modern syllabification, and standardizing alternative spellings and punctuation), but choices have been made regarding possible ways of applying them to the music. Verse 1 has been retained for the five-part version; verse 2 is set to the mildly-ornamented version originally published only as a treble tune, but here given as an alternate reading of the cantus part to be sung upon repetition of the air; verse 4 is supplied as a highly-ornamented treble setting (embellished by the editor in the French manner) and added to the end of the five-part version, as an optional repetition for solo voice (with lute); and verse 3 is found, without a setting, at the end of the edition, to be used if and as the performer wishes, should all four verses be sung.

Certainly, a modern performing edition would not normally be provided with an extended essay (such as the present one), nor with a facsimile reproduction of an entire source. Rather, a prefatory statement would be added, giving information of the performing tradition that the transcription is meant to reflect, clarifying options available, and furnishing enough background to help assure success in performance. Indeed, a modern transcription serves little practical purpose if it does no more than reproduce the pitches found in the original, especially if that original was designed to function as the basis for improvisation.

A few final comments are reserved for certain features of Boësset's air generally not typical of the *air de cour* and, therefore, of special interest. Normally, both halves of an air are repeated, with embellishment. "Je voudrois bien, ô Cloris" has the first repeat written out with some metrical changes and, in the part-song version, with two added voices; the second section constitutes a refrain with an added fifth voice. In fact, the form of the piece relates closely to the texture of constantly-added voice parts; in the five-part version, the work begins à 2, becomes à 4 at the written-out repetition, and à 5 within the refrain—in the shape of a textural crescendo.

Also of interest in this air is the upbeat nature of the opening, which becomes clear only upon examination of the written-out repeat of the first phrase (measure 8). The lute part supplied by Bataille follows the vocal bass of the part-song version almost exactly (which is usual). However, it does not follow the inner parts so closely, often tending to be independent, while providing necessary rhythmic motion and chord tones not present in the voices. All told, the work proves to be an especially attractive example of the early *air de cour*.

BIBLIOGRAPHY

Bacilly, Bénigne de. *Remarques curieuses sur l'Art de bien chanter* (Paris: C. Blageart, 1668). Reissued in an English ed. by Austin B. Caswell, as *A Commentary upon the Art of Proper Singing.* Brooklyn, N.Y.: The Institute of Mediaeval Music, 1968.

Cohen, Albert. "*L'Art de bien chanter* (1666) of Jean Millet." *The Musical Quarterly*, Vol. LV/2 (April, 1969), 170-79.

Duckles, Vincent. "Florid Embellishment in English Song of the Late 16th and Early 17th Centuries." *Annals Musicologiques*, Vol. V. Paris: Société de musique d'autrefois, 1957, 329-45.

Gérold, Théodore. *L'Art du chant en France au XVIIe siècle.* Strasbourg: Istra, 1921.

La Laurencie, Lionel de, and Mairy, Adrienne. *Chansons au luth et Airs de cour français du XVIe siècle.* Publications de la Société Française de Musicologie, première série, Vols. 3-4. Paris: E. Droz, 1934.

Verchaly, André. *Airs de cour pour voix et luth (1603-1643).* Publications de la Société Française de Musicologie, première série, Vol. 16. Paris: Heugel, 1961.

Verchaly, A. "La Tablature dans les recueils francais pour chant et luth (1603-1643)," in *Le Luth et sa musique,* ed. Jean Jacquot. Paris: Centre National de la Recherche Scientifique, 1958, pp. 155-169.

Warlock, Peter. *The English Ayre.* London: Oxford University Press, 1926.

Je voudrois bien, ô Cloris

Antoine Boësset
ed. by Albert Cohen

Verse 4

Cantus

Can it then   bee,   ye   Gods   whom   I   im - por -
Ius-ques à   quand   ô   Dieux!   que   j'im -   por - tu -

- tune,   That   the   Day's   birth   should   make   Love's
- ne   Le   jour   nais - sant   mes   plai - sirs

Morn - ing   die?   And,   this   first   downe   of   my   yet   ten -
des - trui - ra,   Et   les   ef - fets   de   ma   bon - ne

- der   For - tune,   Must   it   make
for - tu - ne   S'en - fui - ront -

wing,   be - cause   fledg'd   Night   doth   flie?
ils   quand   la   nuit   s'en - fui - ra?

Clo - ris!   fare-well;   Oh!   let   mee   dy - ing   van -
A - dieu   Clo - ris,   il   est   temps   que   je   meu -

ish;   Day - light   is   come   my   de - light
re,   La   nuit   s'en   va   et   l'en - nuy

hence   to   ban -   ish.
me   de - meu -   re.

Verse 3

Trustie Night! that, in favour of close Lovers,
Friendly displayest thy securing vailes,
Fright backe pale Morne; tell her thy shadie covers
Can light us best to Love's secret assailes.

Cloris! farewell; Oh! let mee dying vanish;
Day-light is come my delight hence to banish.

O douce nuit de qui les voiles sombres
Sont desployés en faveur des amants,
Ou t' enfuis-tu, scays-tu pas que tes ombres
Donnent la vie à mes contentements?

Adieu Cloris, il est temps que je meure,
La nuit s'en va et l'ennui me demeure.

8

Some Problems of Transcribing Music with Many Sources: The Verse Anthem
O Praise God in His Holiness by Edward Smith

J. BUNKER CLARK
UNIVERSITY OF KANSAS

Edward Smith's verse anthem *O Praise God in His Holiness* incorporates a number of the problems found in transcribing Anglican church music of the first half of the seventeenth century. In spite of the great destruction of music manuscripts during the English Civil War in the 1640s, there are still a multitude of manuscript sources for a composition. An editor needs to determine, if possible, which sources are closest to the composer. In this case, there is no particular problem since the Durham Cathedral sources are obviously closest to this Durham composer. Some difficulty arises, however, from the scarcity of information about the composer. *Grove's Dictionary* describes Edward Smith as the son of William Smith, and also as the organist of Durham Cathedral from 1609 to 1611. More recently, John Buttrey[1] has found that William Smith was a seventeenth-century rather than a sixteenth-century composer. Edward Smith, because of signatures in Durham Ms. A. 2[2] (see Plate 2 for one of these) may have even been the copyist of this anthem in the Durham sources. If so, the date "1639" in Ms. A. 2[3] indicates that our composer was active at Durham considerably later than the 1609-11 period mentioned above. Possibly two musicians with the same name are involved.

Even some of the non-Durham manuscripts have close Durham connections. The manuscripts from Peterhouse are connected with Durham through John Cosin, prebendary at Durham Cathedral in 1624-34 and Master of Peterhouse, Cambridge, in 1635-40. One of Cosin's accomplishments at Peterhouse was establishing the chapel music, and Durham musical sources were used in making a portion of the Peterhouse part-books. York Ms. 29. S and British Museum Add. Mss. 30478-9 were copied by Durham scribes.[4] Only

Tenbury Ms. 791, compiled in London for use with John Barnard's *First Book of Selected Church Musick* (1641)[5] and York Minster Mss. M. 1/1-8 S. (the "Gostling" part-books), dating from after the Restoration, are not principal sources.[6]

I should like to suggest steps to follow in transcribing music with many sources, some of which are applicable only to this type of anthem.[7] First, if possible, determine the best set of part-book sources: that which is closest to the composer (in this case, the Durham manuscripts), or the most reliable (in other English church music of this period, John Barnard's 1641 publication or his manuscript part-books, Royal College of Music Mss. 1045-1051 seem close to many important composers). If there is an organ accompaniment, transcribe it first, leaving room for the voice parts. Transcribe the voice parts by beginning with the bass and progressing up to the soprano. Since *decani* parts (written for the half of the choir on the right, facing the altar) are often higher than the *cantoris*, let the latter precede the former. This avoids later discoveries of additional voice parts that necessitate recopying the score to make room.

Before transcribing from a source, it is useful to copy basic information that often prevents later problems. I put this information for each voice part on a separate slip of paper. The description of the part for a particular part-book (such as 1st Contratenor decani) is necessary if the composer intends to pit the decani side against the cantoris. The inclusive folio or page numbers are useful if a microfilm is to be ordered later. Copy the title of the work and the name of the composer as these appear in each part-book—misattributions are sometimes thereby prevented. Make a note of the measure numbers of solo verses found in a part-book, and any unusual changes such as a 1st

PLATE 1

Durham Cathedral, Ms. C. 4, page 75. The original is unclear, with ink showing through from the back.

PLATE 2
Durham Cathedral, Ms. A. 2, page 359.

PLATE 3
Tenbury, St. Michael's College, Ms. 791 (the "Batten" organ book), folio 245.

Contratenor part becoming what was previously transcribed as the 2nd Contratenor. When, for example, an accidental is found in a source transcribed later, one can thereby easily determine the sources previously used for a voice part or solo section in order to make a critical note listing those sources that do not have the accidental.

The erratic placement of bar lines in seventeenth-century English organ accompaniment manuscripts rarely, if ever, imply accentual or metrical changes from their meter signatures. Therefore, the transcriber need only make regular bar lines every four quarter notes (as reduced from original half notes) for ₵, and every six quarter notes for triple meter. The last note of a section can be regularized as a half or whole note, to fill the measure, assuming that fermatas are used in the sources (for example, see measures 28 and 95). Occasionally, regular barring is not possible—for example, when there are nine quarter notes in triple meter before a change to ₵. In this case, one 9/4 measure is required (see measures 91-2; also measures 84-5). Sections will often end at the middle of a measure; to be honest, the transcriber should not add editorial fermatas unless there is at least one in the sources.

How does one make critical notes, and about what? Listing them on a page as one works often turns out to be messy and confusing, as does putting them as footnotes on the music manuscript paper. The best system seems to be small slips of paper. I put the measure number or numbers on top left, the part name on top center, and the sources concerned listed beginning on top right. The Helmholtz system of pitch nomenclature (middle C is c') should be used, since G = C may be interpreted as $g' = c''$ as well as $g' = c'$. Making critical notes for varying text underlays is time-consuming and tedious, but probably is necessary to reveal an underlay shown in a majority of sources. Since underlay is sometimes haphazard in the manuscripts, it is even advisable to note the absence of a text-slur because such an absence can later prove significant. On the slips of paper, I write the varying text, with note values, slurs, and bar lines underneath.

Organ accompaniments in two or more sources invite a somewhat different treatment. Again, choose one of them as the basis for the organ part. This part, once transcribed, needs to be compared with the others and important differences—pitch and presence or absence of accidentals—noted. Otherwise, it is probably the most practical to conflate the organ sources, using inner parts from one or the other, and rhythms (such as two half notes in place of a whole) that more nearly conform to the voices, without critical comment. Such rhythmic differences, for demonstration, are described in the critical commentary accompanying this anthem. Usually there are so many differences between the organ sources that it is fruitless to describe them all. The relatively small list of critical notes for this anthem is atypical.

With a sizeable number of total sources, the amount of detail necessary for a scholarly edition is sometimes overwhelming. Such detail, however, is not as demanding as deciding which critical notes to omit for a publisher with his eye on the costs of production. There seems to be a national disparity between the thoroughness of scholars in the German tradition who include every small detail of difference between sources, and some English editors who would not describe "obvious errors,"[8] but only those discrepancies of some doubt. The English would maintain that few are likely to read the critical commentary to justify the expense of printing a sizeable one, and that anyone making an extensive study of an edition needs to consult the original sources anyway. I would maintain that an editor, in either case, must prepare for himself detailed critical notes in order to be able to achieve the most satisfactory result. In addition, the more detail printed in the critical commentary, the better. The critical reader is therefore provided the assurance, in print, that the editor has indeed recognized the small discrepancies between sources.

If the publisher applies pressure to keep the critical notes at a minimum, they might be eliminated in this order: (1) critical notes citing the absence of fermatas and differing note values at the end of sections, and the absence of text slurs; (2) varying text underlays. Such a hierarchy is shown in the accompanying critical commentary. Eliminating one or both of these aspects will save much print. The more one omits critical notes, however, the less the edition will be scholarly. If a publisher wishes still more reduction, the editor will have to reserve his critical commentary to the principal set of part-books.

In this edition, text repetitions indicated by repeat signs in the sources are supplied in square brackets. Another method is to use italics. Text outside square brackets derives from at least one source. Text slurs are also from at least one source, and their absence in others is noted in the critical commentary. English church music of this period is usually pitched somewhat low, so the anthem has been transposed upwards. The sketchy organ part has been thickened, and the added notes printed small. (It is a convention to indicate for the publisher in red anything to be printed with small type.) I prefer to place editorial accidentals before the note, printed small or in square brackets, rather than above the note. Precautionary accidentals may be shown with regular parentheses. Presumably, in other types of music, the placement of accidentals above the note may be reserved for optional editorial accidentals. Unfortunately, this particular anthem is devoid of problems of accidentals. Others of this period display cross relationships that demand many editorial judgments.

NOTES

1. "William Smith of Durham," *Music & Letters*, XLIII (July, 1962), 248-254.

2. "Edw: Smith" on pp. 1, 272, and 359; "Edward Smythe" on p. 274.

3. On p. 162.

4. See Wyn K. Ford, "An English Liturgical Part-book of the 17th Century," *Journal of the American Musicological Society*, XII (Summer-Fall, 1959), 144-160.

5. See my article "Adrian Batten and John Barnard: Colleagues and Collaborators," *Musica Disciplina*, XXII (1968), 207-229.

6. Sources of the period are discussed in Peter le Huray, "Towards a Definitive Study of Pre-Restoration Anglican Service Music," *Musica Disciplina*, XIV (1960), 167-195.

7. See Peter le Huray, *Music and the Reformation in England 1549-1660* (London: Herbert Jenkins, 1967), p. 106, for one voice line as it differs in eleven sources.

8. *Editing Early Music*, by Thurston Dart, Walter Emery, and Christopher Morris (London: Novello, Oxford University Press, and Stainer & Bell, 1963), p. 9. This is an excellent guide for editors, and is inexpensive as well.

ACKNOWLEDGMENTS

The Trustees of the British Museum
The Warden and Fellows of St. Michael's College, Tenbury
The Dean and Chapter of Durham Cathedral
The Master and Fellows of Peterhouse, Cambridge
Lt. Col. Sir John Dunnington-Jefferson, owner of Ms. M. 29. S., deposited at York Minster
The Dean and Chapter of York Minster

O Praise God in His Holiness

Edward Smith
ed. by J. Bunker Clark

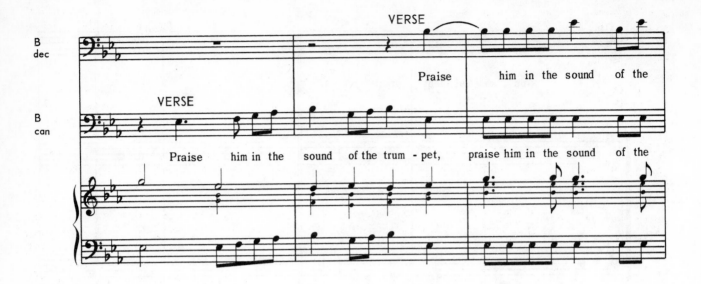

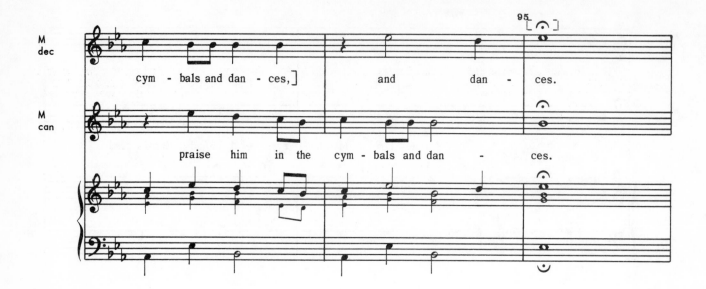

TEXT: Psalm 150, verses 1-6, *Book of Common Prayer*

VOCAL SOURCES

Medius decani

Cambridge, Peterhouse, Ms. 475 (Medius decani) (Cp 475), f. 135: "Smith, O praise god in his holinesse. Medius Decany." Verse, meas. 78-95.

Medius cantoris

Cambridge, Peterhouse, Ms. 479 (Medius cantoris) (Cp 479), f. 136v: "Mr Edward Smyth, O prayse god in his holinesse." Verse, meas. 80-95.

Durham Cathedral, Ms. C. 1 (Medius) (Dc1), pp. 44-45: "Mr Edw: Smith, O praise god in his holynes." Verse, meas. 80-95.

1st Contratenor

Cambridge, Peterhouse, Ms. 476 (1st Contratenor decani) (Cp 476), f. 146: "Smith, O praise god in his holinesse. Contratenor." All verses.

Durham Cathedral, Ms. C. 6 (1st Contratenor decani) (Dc6), pp. 77-78: "Edward Smith, O praise god in his holynes." All verses.

Durham Cathedral, Ms. C. 7 (1st Contratenor cantoris) (Dc7), pp. 291-292: "O praise &c."

York Minster, Contratenor decani (Y-c), pp. 154-155: "Ed: Smith, O praise God in his holines." All verses.

2nd Contratenor

Cambridge, Peterhouse, Ms. 480, (1st Contratenor cantoris) (Cp 480), f. 126: "Smith, O praise god in his holinesse. Contratenor Decany ["Cantoris" crossed out]."

Durham Cathedral, Ms. C. 4 (2nd Contratenor decani) (Dc4), p. 75: "Edward Smith, O praise God in his holynes."

Durham Cathedral, Ms. C. 5 (2nd Contratenor cantoris) (Dc5), p. 73: "Mr: Edward Smith, O praise God in his holines &c."

York Minster, Contratenor cantoris (Y-d), p. 156: "Edm: Smith, O praise God in his holines &c."

Tenor decani

Durham Cathedral, Ms. C. 9 (Tenor decani) (Dc9), pp. 49-50: "Edward Smith, O praise god in his holynes."

Durham Cathedral, Ms. C. 11, verso (Tenor decani) (Dc11v), pp. 183-184: "Edward Smith, O praise god in his holyness."

York Minster, Tenor decani (Y-e), p. 144: "Ed: Smith, O praise God in his holines." Verses, meas. 5-19 (Bass cantoris, with clef F-4), 31-52 (Tenor cantoris), 68-76 (Bass decani, clef F-4), 111-124 (Bass decani, clef F-4).

Tenor cantoris

Cambridge, Peterhouse, Ms. 490 (Tenor cantoris) (Cp 490), ff. K2-K2v: "Smith, O praise god in his holinesse. Tenor cantoris." All verses.

Durham Cathedral, Ms. C. 10 (Tenor cantoris) (Dc10), pp. 64-65: "Mr Edward Smith, O praise God in his holines &c." All verses.

London, British Museum, Add. Ms. 30478 (Tenor cantoris) (Lb78), ff. 134-135: "Mr Edward Smith, O praise god in his holyness. psal. 150." All verses. Key signature: 1 flat; all B's are therefore flat.

London, British Museum, Add. Ms. 30479 (Tenor cantoris) (Lb79), ff. 99v-100v: "Mr Edward Smith, O Praise god in his holines." All verses.

Bass decani

Cambridge, Peterhouse, Ms. 478 (Bass decani) (Cp 478), ff. 162-162v: "O prayse God in his holyness." All verses.

Cambridge, Peterhouse, Ms. 488 (Bass decani) (Cp 488), ff. H1v-H2: "O prayse god in his holyness &c." All verses.

Durham Cathedral, Ms. C. 16 (Bass) (Dc16), pp. 151-153: "Mr: Smith, O praise God in his holynes." Verse, meas. 68-76.

Durham Cathedral, Ms. C. 19 (Bass) (Dc19), pp. 189-190: "Edward Smith, O praise god in his holynes." All verses.

York Minster, Ms. M. 29. S (Bass decani) (Y29), pp. 122-123: "Mr Edward Smith, O praise God in his holynes." All verses.

Bass cantoris

Cambridge, Peterhouse, Ms. 481 (Bass cantoris) (Cp 481), f. 123: "Smith, O praise god in his holinesse. Bassus Cantoris." All verses.

Durham Cathedral, Ms. C. 17 (Bass) (Dc17), pp. 136-137: "Mr Ed: Smith, O Praise God in his." All verses.

The critical notes follow this form: measure number(s) and the number of the beat within the measure; voice part; manuscript by symbol: the variant reading. Symbols for note values are: W = whole, H = half, Q = quarter, E = eighth, S = sixteenth. A dot following the note value indicates a dotted note, as H. = dotted half. Hyphens connecting the symbols refer to text slurs, as H-Q-Q H means the first three notes serve for one text syllable. Asterisks indicate the priority of importance of the critical notes. Two asterisks accompany those notes that should not be omitted, one means the note that could possibly be omitted, none shows those that are probably dispensable.

**12,2; Bass can; Y-e: *a* no ♮

  22,4-23,2; Bass can; Dc17: no slur

**24,1; Medius; Dc1: Q = E E

*25,3-26; Medius; Cp 475, Cp 479: H H Q.-E = W Q. E.

  27,3½-28,1; 2nd Ct; Cp 480, Dc4: no slur

  27,4-28,2; Medius; Cp 475, Cp 479: no slur

  28,3; all but Dc1 (Medius) and Dc17 (Bass): H = W

  28,3; 1st Ct (Cp 476, Y-c), 2nd Ct (Cp 480, Y-d), Tenor (Cp 490), Bass (Cp 481, Cp 488, Dc16, Y29): no fermata

**35,2-36,2; 1st Ct dec; Y-c: "praise him in his" H-rest Q Q E E

**37,4; Tenor can; Lb78: *c'* Q = H.

52,3; 1st Ct (Cp476, Y-c), Tenor (Lb79, Y-e): no fermata

**55-56,1; 1st Ct; Cp476: H. H = H H.

57,3-4; Tenor; Lb78: no slur

*62-64,2; 1st Ct; Y-c: "praise [him ac-cord-ing to his ex-cel-lent great-]" H Q. E Q Q E E Q E E Q

**63,1; Bass can; Dc17: E E = E. S

63,4-64,2; 2nd Ct; Dc5: no slur

63,4-64,2; 1st Ct; Cp 476: no slur

**64,2; 2nd Ct; Dc4, Dc5: *d'* ♮

64,3; all but Cp 480 (2nd Ct): H = W

64,3; Medius (Cp 475, Dc1), 1st Ct (Cp 476, Y-c), 2nd Ct (Y-d), Bass (Cp 488, Dc16, Y29): no fermata

**76,3; Tenor (Cp 490, Dc10, Lb78), Bass dec (Dc19, Y-e): fermata

95; Medius dec (Cp 475), Medius can (Cp1-b, Dc1): W = H

95; Medius can; Dc1: no fermata

*100,2-3; 1st Ct; Cp 476, Dc7, Y-c: E E-Q = E-E Q

**100, 3; Medius; Dc1: *d''* = *b'*

**100,3-4; Tenor; Dc9, Dc11v, Y-e: Q Q = Q. E

**103,1-2; 1st Ct; Y-c: *e' f' g' = g' a' b'*

103,3½-4; 2nd Ct; Cp 480: no slur

**104,4½; Medius; Dc1: *c''* = *b'*

*106,1½-107,1; 1st Ct; Dc7, Y-c: E E-E E-H. = E E-E-E H.

106,1½-107,4; 1st Ct; Cp 476: no slurs

106,2-3; 2nd Ct; Cp 480: no slur

106,3½-4; Tenor; Cp 490, Dc10: no slur

108; 1st Ct; Cp 476, Dc6: W = H

108; 1st Ct (Cp 476, Y-c), 2nd Ct (Cp 480, Y-d), Tenor (Y-e), Bass (Cp 481, Cp 488, Dc16, Y29): no fermata

**113,3-114,1; Bass dec; Y-e: *f e* H H = *f g* Q Q

**114,1; Bass dec; Dc16, Y29: *e = g*

**115,4-119,3; Bass dec; Y-e: missing

**119,4; Bass dec; Dc16: *g = c' (c'* erased)

*120,4-121,2; Bass dec; Dc16, Dc19, Y29: Q. E-E-Q = Q E-S-S-Q (no slur in Dc19)

121,1½-2; Bass dec; Y-e: no slur

124; Bass dec; Cp 478, Cp 488, Dc16, Dc19, Y-e, Y29: W = H

*126-127; Tenor; Dc9, Dc11v Y-e: *b b a b* = H H W

*126,3-129,2; Bass dec; Dc16, Dc19, Y29: H-W W Q Q = H W W H

*126,3-127,1; 1st Ct; Cp 476, Y-c, Dc7: Q. E-H = Q.-E H (no slur in Dc7)

*126,3-127,1; 2nd Ct; Cp 480, Dc5, Y-d: Q. E-Q = Q.-E Q

*127,3½-130,2; 2nd Ct; Dc4, Dc5: "the" E-Q-Q-Q-Q-Q-Q.-E-Q.-E-Q-Q (no slur in Dc4)

*127,3½-130,2; 2nd Ct; Cp 480: "the Lord" E Q-Q-Q-Q "praise" Q "[the Lord]" Q. E Q. E Q Q H

*127,4-129,2; 1st Ct; Cp 476, Dc6, Dc7: "praise" Q. "the" E Q Q H Q

**128,1; Tenor; Cp 490: *b* has fermata

*128,2-129,1; Bass can; Cp 481: Q. E-Q-H = Q.-E-Q H

**128,3-129,3; Tenor; all sources: H-rest H-rest Q-rest = Q-rest

*128,4-131,2; Tenor; Dc9, Dc11v: "praise the" Q. E-Q-H-E-E-Q-H-Q-Q (no slur in Dc9)

*129,2-130; Medius; Cp 475: "praise the" Q.-E-Q-Q-H Q

**129,2½-3; 2nd Ct; Dc5:♮ on *g'* instead of *a'*

*130-131,1; Tenor; Y-e: "that hath breath praise" E E-Q Q. E-Q

*130-1½-131,2; Tenor; Dc10, Lb78, Lb79: "the" E-Q-H-Q-Q

*131,2-133,1; 1st Ct; Cp 476, Dc6, Dc7: "praise" Q "the" E Q Q Q Q H

*131,4-133; 2nd Ct; Cp 480: "praise [the Lord]"

*132-134,1; Bass can; Dc17: W. H-H W = W.-H H-H H

**132,1-133,3; Tenor; Lb78: missing

*132,1½-134,2; 2nd Ct; Dc4, Dc5: "the" E-Q-Q-H-Q (no slur in Dc4)

*132,2-135,2; Bass dec; Dc16, Y29: "praise the Lord, praise the" Q. E-Q-H-H-H Q Q. E-Q

*132,2-135,2; Bass dec; Dc19: "praise the Lord, praise the" Q. E Q-H-H-H-Q Q. E-Q

*133,4-135,1; Medius; Cp 479: "praise the" Q. E-Q-W

**134; Bass dec; Cp 478: ♮ added to *A* in later hand

**134; Bass dec; Cp 488: *A* and *B* ♮

*134-135,2; Bass dec; Cp 488: "the Lord, praise the" H Q Q. E-Q

134,3-135; Tenor; Cp 490, Dc10, Dc11v, Lb78, Lb79, Y-e: H-W = W

134,3-135,2; 2nd Ct; Cp 480, Dc4: no slur

134,4-135,1; 1st Ct; Cp 476: no slur

135,3; all but Tenor; all: H = W

135,3; Medius (Cp 475, Dc1), 1st Ct (Cp 476, Y-c), 2nd Ct (Cp 480), Tenor (Lb78, Lb79), Bass (Cp 478, Dc16, Y29): no fermata

136-137; Bass dec; Cp 478, Y29: no slur

*136-138; 1st Ct; Cp 476, Dc6, Dc7: "A-" W Q. E Q Q Q H Q

*136-140,2; 2nd Ct; Cp 480, Dc5: one "A-men"

*136-142; Bass dec; Dc19: one "A-men"

*136-141; Bass dec; Dc16: "A-" W W W "-men" H E E Q W "-men" Q "A-" Q. E Q (sic)

*137-139; Medius; Dc1: W W W = "A-men" W. W

**137,2; Tenor; Cp 490, Dc10, Lb78, Lb79: *b = c'*

*139-141; Bass dec; Y29: "A-" H E E "A-men" Q W "A-" Q Q. E Q (sic)

*139-140; 2nd Ct; Cp 480: "-men" Q. E "A-" Q Q H H (sic)

*139-141; Bass dec; Cp 478: "A-" H E E Q "-men" W "A-" Q. E Q

**141,2; Tenor; Y-e: H Q = H.

*142; Bass dec; Dc16, Dc19, Y29: *e g b = e*

142; Medius (Cp 475), 1st Ct (Cp 476), 2nd Ct (Cp 480), Bass dec (Cp 488, Dc16, Y29), Bass can (Cp 481): no fermata

ORGAN

Tenbury Ms. 791 (T791), ff. 245-247: "Edward Smith, O Praise god in his holynes."

Durham Cathedral, Ms. A. 2 (Da2), pp. 359-362: "Edw. Smith, O praise god in his holynes."

Durham Cathedral, Ms. A. 5 (Da5), pp. 90-94: "Mr: Edward Smith, O praise god in his holynes."

*1; Da2: upper clef C-2

*1; Da5: upper clef G-3, lower clef F-4

*5,3; T791, Da2: lower clef F-4

**12,2; T791: *a* no ♮

**14,4; T791: *d* has ♮

*18,3-19,2; T791: *B* H H = H. Q

*19,3-20,1; T791: *e* H. = H Q

*21,3-4; Da5: *f g* Q. E = Q E E

28,3; T791, Da2: H = W

*29,1; Da2: lower clef C-4

*31,1; T791: *d'* has ♮

*31,3; Da2: lower clef F-4

*32; T791: *e* H H = W

*43,1½; T791: *a'* E. S = Q

*43,3½-4; T791: *b'* E E = Q

**43,4; T791: *e'* = *g'*

*57,3-58,1; T791: *e* H. = H Q

**59,3; T791: *b* Q = *f b* E E

**63,1; T791: *f g* is in previous measure, has an extra *a* Q instead

64,3; all: H = W

*65,1; all: lower clef C-4

*67; all: lower clef F-4

**69,1-2; T791: *e* E E E E = Q Q. E E E and *g''* Q. E = Q Q. E E E

*76,4-77,1; T791: *e'* H = Q Q

**77,4; T791: bass is *c'*, tenor is *e'*

**84,3; Da2, T791: *A* = *B*

*85,1; T791: meter C

95; all: W=H

**101,2; T791: *b'* = *c''*

**106,3-4; T791: *b'* H = *d''* *b'* Q Q

**115,3; T791: *a* = *c'*

**121,3-4; Da5: *B* and *d''* missing

**123,1; T791, Da2: *a b* E E = *a* Q

**123,1-2; Da5: *A e* = *f e* Q E-rest E

124; all: W = H

*128; Da2, Da5: *B* W = H H

**128; Da2: tenor *b a g* Q. E Q Q-rest

*129,3-130,2; Da2, Da5: *f* W = H H

*131-132; Da2, Da5: *b'* W W = H H H H

*132; Da2, Da5: *B* W = H H

*134,3-135,2; Da2, Da5: *b'* W = H H

135,3; all: H = W

135,3; T791: no fermata

*136; Da2, Da5: *A* W = H H

*137-138; Da2, Da5: *b'* W W = H H H H

*138; Da5: *B* W = H H

*140; Da2, Da5: *A* W = H H

*141; Da2, Da5: *b'* W = H H and *B* W = H Q. E

9

English Consort Music:
Fancy and Ayre in G Minor (c. 1660)
by John Jenkins (1592-1678)

ROBERT AUSTIN WARNER
THE UNIVERSITY OF MICHIGAN

The music of John Jenkins and contemporaneous composers of the great indigenous school of English chamber music for strings is just emerging from the archives. Preserved principally in the larger libraries of Great Britain, this music generally remains in part-books copied by those who wished to perform it. Scores are an exception, holographs rare, and copyists usually unknown. Since pieces frequently exist in multiple sources which usually differ, any information which establishes greater authority for a given manuscript is extremely significant. Consequently, studies dealing with the manuscripts themselves are of the highest importance to an editor.[1] Lacking the information such studies reveal, the choice among variants must rest on internal evidence, that is, on the consistency of a variant to the general musical style. Such a process involves penetrating analytical study and frequent reevaluation of variants as knowledge of either style or external factors accumulates.

In general, the manuscripts give only a minimum of information: (1) a title, usually generic, such as Almand or Fancy; (2) the name of the composer; (3) parts identified by range, such as cantus, first treble, or bass; (4) a clef; (5) a key signature; (6) a time signature; (7) the notes; and (8) accidentals. Even all of these features are not always present. In addition, bar lines are written in keyboard parts but function only as visual aids to divide the notes into groups small enough to be easily perceived. The number of beats in such "measures" may consequently vary with the activity of the part and relate to time signatures only in that duple and triple time are evident by their placement. Probably not the copyists but various performers inserted the bar lines which are sometimes found in other parts. Their form, bisecting long notes and usually extending beyond the limits of the staff suggest a hurried later addition. Furthermore, they are frequently found in one part and not in another within the same manuscript. Consequently, the inclusion of original barring serves no musical or scholarly purpose, and an edition can profit by the regular bar lines with which contemporary musicians are most comfortable. In addition to these features, title pages in some cases reveal the actual names of instruments desired. The keyboard instrument at least is usually identified. Sometimes dates, presumably recording the time of the finished copy, are given. Furthermore, particularly in the later works, an occasional dynamic, ornamental sign, fingering, or tempo indication may be found, again giving evidence of addition by individual performers.

The notation itself offers relatively few problems; and if those were not explained sufficiently by Fellowes years ago, they could be rediscovered by study and deduction.[2] In manuscripts seen by this writer, key signatures range between three flats and three sharps with minor keys in flats frequently designated by the Dorian signature. Accidentals affect only the notes by which they appear unless another note of the same pitch follows immediately. Minor exceptions are easily identified. Without the availability of the natural sign, a flat contradicts a previous sharp and vice versa. Occasionally, precautionary accidentals are inserted, but more often, such care is lacking. Collation between manuscripts usually shows many deviations in accidentals as well as frequent variants in the notes themselves.

Usually the quarter note is the unit of the beat, but in some of the earlier music especially, and particularly in triple time, larger units may suggest possible reduction for modern editions. Duple time is, in this writer's observation, universally indicated by C. The modern equivalent is more frequently $\frac{4}{4}$ than $\frac{2}{2}$, but only the study of the rhythmic flow of individual pieces can give a reasonably positive answer. Triple time may be indicated by many methods: 3, 31, 3i, $\frac{i}{3}$, $\frac{C}{3}$, and ϕ $\frac{i}{3}$. Since different triple signatures may be found in the same place in different part-books, they are obviously interchangeable. Ravenscroft, in deploring the abandonment of the older proportional signatures, relates the irrational practice of his period, a practice which later English theorists accepted without quibbling.[3] Proportion is not entirely dead, however. A sesquialtera relation between duple and triple time is often appropriate, but some editors understandably prefer simply to indicate a faster tempo for triple time. Often in the latter part of the period, some tempo shift seems appropriate between major sections of duple time, and now and then the word Drag or Slow may appear in one or more part-books at the final section of a fancy, which implies that performers were accustomed to making such changes without any specific indication and only wrote in the words when memory failed.[4] In general, modern performers will find a moderate tempo, regulated by the practical speed of the most rapid passages, suitable for these pieces.

That dynamic variety was expected from performers is obvious from several sources in the period. Perhaps most relevant to the present edition are the instructions written by a performer on some dance-derived pieces of Jenkins in a manuscript now owned by the Newberry Library.[5] The instructions dealing with repeated strains solve no problems for the Jenkins' fancies, which do not have repeated sections, but they are obviously applicable to the airs; and the dynamic principles, involving contrasting dynamics on repeats, may well be applied with suitable care within the fancies of this late period. Regardless of this "humouring," however, dynamics in individual parts should follow the rise and fall of the melodic line, an interpretation possible only when a basic fortissimo is avoided; and thematic material must be prominent but not overpowering within the polyphonic ensemble. Divisions sparkle when the basic dynamic is soft, while the final sections often respond to a rich, full sound. Nevertheless, opportunities for effective echo effects and other dynamic contrast appropriate to the Baroque should not be overlooked.[6]

Slurs are extremely rare. The few appearances in some manuscripts are usually combinations of two-eighth or two-sixteenth notes, which may imply that slurrings of small groups were used much oftener than performers indicated. Arnold Ashbee suggests that they may indicate inequality in note lengths, a creditable hypothesis that would nevertheless not exclude the possibility of maintaining the actual slur.[7] When cadential trills and shaked elevations in thirty-second notes occur, slurring would appear inevitable in order both to fulfill the function of the ornament and to facilitate technic.[8] The accompanying edition, however, includes no editorial bowing indications, for bowing among perceptive and reasonably informed performers becomes a highly personal matter. A linked bowing, for instance, may be used for convenience without altering articulation.

Ornaments described in contemporaneous English treatises can be applied if they emerge in good taste. Although many pieces require little added motion, simple turns or cadential trills are frequently needed. The vibrato, called the "closed shake" by Christopher Simpson, was considered an appropriate device to embellish a long note.[9] Tempo, dynamics, bowings, and ornaments all deserve careful thought and intelligent experimentation.

Worthy of mention if only to avoid confusion is the sign of congruence, frequently found as three or more dots at a cadence or at a new point of imitation. Such signs are superfluous in a modern edition when regular bars and numbered measures perform their task more efficiently. Dots on either side of double bars, which occur in Ayres or dance-derived movements, pose an interesting question, for they may be purely decorative.[10] Sometimes a repetition was indicated by the figure 2 over the double bar. Various written sources, however, tell us that such strains were normally repeated and usually varied by dynamics, ornaments, or even more elaborate methods. The custom is more definitive than the actual dots, which in contemporary practice are used to indicate repeats.

Obviously the organ parts of the period caused few problems to performers, for no source yet discovered describes the usage.[11] The customary part contains an unfigured bass along with various notes assembled from the upper parts and placed within reach of the hands on two six-lined staves. The bass is musically logical; the upper parts appear only to provide the player with a sketch of what is going on and sometimes to indicate inversions of chords. By the time of late Jenkins, a

First Treble   **Second Treble**

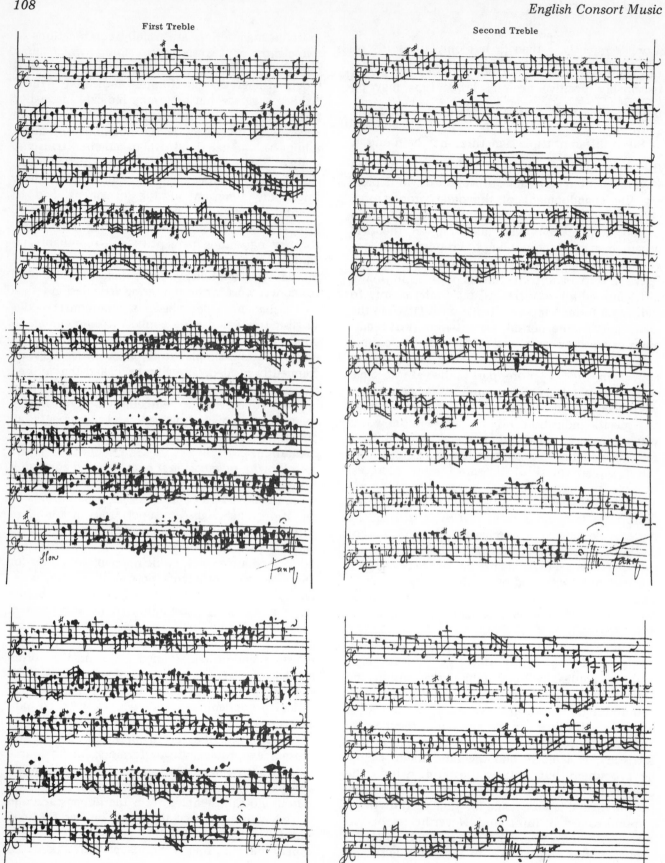

Parts for the "Fancy and Ayre in G Minor" by John Jenkins, Nos. 13 and 14 in the Oxford Bodleian Music School manuscript, folios 564-567.

sparsely figured thorough bass replaces the organ bass, but even then occasional closely-spaced chords in the bass are reminiscent of the earlier devices. The present writer has made careful editorial additions to Jenkins' organ basses with instructions to the performer to elaborate or even delete, depending on the instrument used and on the musical situation.[12] The actual thorough bass parts are less problematical. With the minimal information provided by the two English treatises dealing with thorough bass, combined with a general knowledge of the Italian heritage, a satisfactory solution can be found. The suggestions of Matthew Locke have been especially useful to this editor, particularly his device of accompanying scalar passages in the bass with parallel thirds.[13] The practice derives from similar usage in the string parts. The continuo part must always be adapted to the strength of the medium and the qualities of the instrument used is realization. Perhaps a chamber organ could play the editor's realizations with few changes, but the same parts performed on a harpsichord would need filled-in chords and arpeggiation at various places for proper emphasis. In conformity with earlier continuo practice, the performer should deliberately use more than one

VARIANT READINGS: FANCY AND AYRE IN G

Measure	Part	Beat	Note	Deviation	Source
				FANCY	
1	Bass	4	2	*e*-flat	OB, BM
6	Tr. I	3	1	*b″*-flat	BM
6	Tr. I	4	1	*d‴*	OB, BM
10	Cont.	2	2	*e*-flat	BM
24	Cont.	2	2	*c*	BM
37	Tr. I	3	2	♪	BM
38	Bass	1	5	*e*-flat, no sharp	OB, BM
50	Cont.	3	2	*B*-flat	OB, BM
52	Tr. I Cont.			Time signature $\frac{i}{3}$	BM
52	Bass			Time signature 3	BM
52	Tr. II			Time signature $\phi\frac{i}{3}$	BM
52	All			Time signature 3i	OB
61	Tr. II	2-3		rhythm, two quarters	BM
62	All			Time signature ₵	BM, OB
62	Tr. II Cont.			"slow" not indicated	OB, BM
				AYRE	
5	Tr. II	3	2	*a*	BM
11	Tr. I	2			OB
13-14	Tr. I			Double bar only	BM
13-14	Tr. II			2 over double bar, dots on right only	BM
13-14	Bass			2 over double bar, no dots	BM
13-14	All Parts			Double bar only	OB
18	Cont.	1		3-flat written over sharp	OB

vertical note in the left hand when richness is needed in the accompaniment.

The present edition is based primarily on the Oxford Bodleian manuscript presented above, which appears to be the more accurate of the two extant sources, the other source being manuscript. Additional 27550-54 (Nos. 23 and 24) in the British Museum. Neither source is autograph, nor can the copyists be identified except for John Lilly, a professional musician and friend of Jenkins, who wrote out the first treble part in the British Museum copy.[14] Both manuscripts, however, show careful regard for legibility, and only the penetration of ink through the pages mars their clarity in reproduction. The present edition allows reconstruction of the original sources by showing deviations in the collation table.

Neither manuscript names the intended stringed instruments. Yet, the answer is obvious. A treble range frequently exceeding a'', the top fret of the treble viol, and characterized by much activity points convincingly to the use of violins, instruments far more brilliant than viols particularly in the upper range. On the other hand, the double stops in the bass part in measures 38 and 41, and the general configuration of the rapid divisions are much more characteristic of the bass viola da gamba, regardless of whether or not they are possible to play on the cello. In spite of the complaints of such a conservative as Thomas Mace, the combination of violins with the bass viol was frequent during the middle years of the seventeenth century.[15] Anthony Wood at mid-century also indicates possible options between keyboard instruments.[16]

Quite commonly, errors have been perpetuated in copying from one manuscript to another without in any way revealing which manuscript was the earlier, or even if both were copied from an unknown earlier manuscript. This situation is illustrated in measure 6, where a probable error (d''' against c'' and e-flat) appears in both first treble parts. Another mutual error is revealed in the continuo in measure 50 by the contradiction in the bass of both manuscripts. Much less obvious and consequently more troublesome is the rhythmic deviation in measure 11 of the Ayre, where this editor eventually chose the version presented by the British Museum manuscript as being more consistent with the general motion of the strain, a decision which strongly implies an acceptance of an unknown third manuscript containing the first error. The manuscript versions in measure 38 would have fit the English style of the earlier viol ensembles, but the cross relation sounds awkward in such tonal surroundings. The editorial natural in the bass part is justified by the premise that the copyist could have easily forgotten the sharp and that the mistake could have been perpetuated in further copies.

A date of 1674 is found at the beginning of the first treble part of the British Museum copy. Jenkins, eighty-two by that date, had doubtless composed the piece years before. Nevertheless, the use of the continuo alone, aside from other stylistic features, places this piece late in Jenkins' output. The suite, then, shows the composer near the end of a long and distinguished development of craft and artistry. In spite of his absorption of both French and Italian influences, he still maintained features of the vital English tradition, which he presented effectively in his own distinctive style.

NOTES

1. See numerous articles by Pamela Willetts, written in the 1960s and published in *Music and Letters*, and *The British Museum Quarterly*; *The Bodleian Library Record*; also Murray Lefkowitz, "The Longleat Papers of Bulstrode Whitelocke," *Journal of the American Musicological Society*, XVIII (1965), 42-60.

2. Edmund Horace Fellowes, *The English Madrigal School*, I (London: Stainer and Bell, 1913), Preface. He enlarges on those features in *The English Madrigal Composers*, 2nd ed. (London: Oxford University Press, 1948), Ch IX.

3. Thomas Ravenscroft, *A Brief Discourse* of the True (but Neglected) use of *Charact'ring* the *Degrees*, (London, 1914), pp. 9-20 in which he discusses the definitions and divisions of mood, time, and prolation.

4. Thomas Mace, *Musick's Monument* (London, 1676), p. 81.

5. Case MX—VM 1 .A 18 J52c. See the analysis of performance indications given by Jane Troy Johnson, "How to 'Humour' John Jenkins' Three-part Dances: Performance Directions in a Newberry Library MS," *Journal of the American Musicological Society*, XX (1967), 197-208.

6. Although these remarks are partially pragmatic, they still stem from hints dropped in various sources. Mace, p. 236, for instance, instructs that no one part should overshadow another. Christopher Simpson, *The Division Viol*, A Lithographic Facsimile of the Second Edition [London, 1665] (London: J. Curwen & Sons, 1955), p. 10, speaks of gracing by the bow. Furthermore, numerous references including the translation of Caccini's *Nuove Musicke* in John Playford, *A Brief Introduction to the Skill of Musick* [1654] (London; 1667), pp. 39-58, speak of expressive nuance either directly or by implication.

7. John Jenkins, *Consort Music of Four Parts*, ed. Arnold Ashbee, *Musica Britannica*, XXVI (London: Stainer and Bell, 1969), xviii.

8. Simpson, pp. 11-12.

9. Simpson, *loc. cit.*

10. Robert Donington, *The Interpretation of Early Music* (London: Faber and Faber, 1963), p. 311, explains the practice and quotes Charles Butler, *Principles of Music* (London, 1636), p. 37, and Playford, the 1674 ed., p. 35, to support his argument.

11. Thurston Dart and William Coates in the Preface to *Jacobean Consort Music*, *Musica Britannica* IX, (London: Stainer and Bell, 1955), xix, state that, in absence of any English theoretical writings to serve as a guide, their additions to "viol continuo" are based in general on the keyboard parts by Coperario.

12. John Jenkins, *Three-Part Fancy and Ayre Divisions*, ed. Robert Austin Warner, No. 10, "The Wellesley Edition" (Wellesley, Mass.: Wellesley College, 1966).

13. Matthew Locke, *Melothesia*, (London, 1673) and Dr. John Blow, British Museum Additional 34072, ff. 1-5, whose rules are published by F. T. Arnold, *The Art of Accompaniment From a Thorough-Bass* (Reprint, 2 vols.) (New York: Dover, 1965), I, 154-72.

14. Pamela J. Willetts, "John Lilly, Musician and Music Copyist," *The Bodleian Library Record*, VII (1967), 307-10.

15. Mace, p. 233.

16. Anthony Wood, *The Life and Times of Anthony Wood*, ed. Andrew Clark (5 vols.) (London: Oxford Historical Society, 1891-1900), I, 212.

Fancy and Ayre in G Minor

John Jenkins
ed. by Robert Austin Warner

10

Some Aspects of Notation in
an *Alma Redemptoris Mater* (c. 1670)
by Marc-Antoine Charpentier (d. 1704)

H. WILEY HITCHCOCK
BROOKLYN COLLEGE OF THE CITY UNIVERSITY OF NEW YORK

The *Alma Redemptoris Mater* by Marc-Antoine Charpentier here considered is one of a number of varied settings of this Marian antiphon by the composer. It exists only in a single manuscript version (see the accompanying facsimile), which is among the "Mélanges autographes" of Charpentier in the Bibliothèque Nationale in Paris (Ms. Rés. Vm 1 259: vol. II, foll. 90ᵛ—92). These twenty-eight volumes are not arranged in chronological order of composition; a better guide to the chronology of the music contained in them is provided by Charpentier's numbering of the *cahiers* (fascicles) of his manuscripts. Essentially, there are two main series of such *cahiers*, one numbered with Arabic numerals, the other with Roman. The two series were not numbered consecutively (the Arabic numeral series first, then the Roman, or vice-versa) but more or less concurrently.[1] *Alma Redemptoris Mater* is found near the beginning of *cahier* 16. This suggests a date in the early 1670s for its composition, since the more or less contemporaneous *cahiers* XV and XVI include precisely datable music of that time—an overture for the first Paris performance of Molière's *La Comtesse d'Escarbagnas* (July 8, 1672) and various pieces for the premiere of *Le Malade imaginaire* (February 10, 1673). Thus, *Alma Redemptoris Mater* is a fairly early work of Charpentier, for he had been in Rome, studying with Carissimi, as late as the mid-1660s.[2]

This dating of the work, early in the composer's career, is borne out by the musical hand of the autograph, which by comparison with that of a late work like the oratorio *Judicium Salomonis* (1702), for instance, is relatively unformed. It is also borne out by aspects of the notation which are distinctly conservative, not to say *retardataires*

(although by no means unique to Charpentier). Indeed, the notation of *Alma Redemptoris Mater* is exactly what we might expect from a young composer fresh from mid-seventeenth-century study in Rome with an older one (Carissimi was born in 1605) who was himself steeped in the scholastic tradition of Roman sacred polyphony and was a master of the *stile antico* of Church music (if also of the newer declamatory and *bel canto* styles).

The aspects of notation which invite some comment here, specifically in relation to questions they raise for a modern edition, have to do with (1) the key-signature, (2) the time-signatures and barring, and (3) the note-shapes.

The key-signature. Like almost all seventeenth-century works with any key-signature at all, this one has one less inflection in its signature than the modern musician expects. This is a legacy from Gregorian chant and its transposed forms. Summarily put, when the Dorian mode was on its way to becoming minor (partly through the consistent flatting of its sixth degree), it preserved for a long time its official character as a diatonic mode, with no flat indicated in the signature. The same was true of Mixolydian as it tended to become major (through consistent sharping of its seventh degree): for a long time, composers failed to indicate the consistency of the leading-tone by acknowledging it in a key-signature. When either the Dorian/minor or the Mixolydian/major was transposed, the result was similarly a signature with one less inflection than was called for by the actual music.

This notational anomaly was maintained generally until the eighteenth century: one familiar instance is Handel's clavier suite in E major (with the "Harmonious Blacksmith" variations), which has only three sharps in the original signature. By

The *Alma Redemptoris Mater* of Marc-Antoine Charpentier (Paris, Bibliothèque Nationale, Ms. Rés. Vm 1 259: vol. II, fol. 90ᵛ-92).

that time, a compatriot and contemporary of Charpentier had already called attention to the anomaly (at least regarding the minor mode), thus signaling its imminent demise. This was Saint-Lambert, who in the preface to his *Nouveau Traité de l'accompagnement* commented that "tout ton qui a le mode mineur a la sixième de sa finale essentiellement mineure" and warned that in his treatise's musical examples he would put the flat "à la clef, et non pas dans le courant de l'air comme accidental, ainsi qu'il se pratique ordinairement; ce qui est une erreur considérable. . . ."[3]

The time-signatures and barring. The time-signatures of *Alma Redemptoris Mater*, and its barring, reveal how precariously mid-seventeenth-century music was poised between two systems of notation—between the proportional notation of the Renaissance and the orthochronic notation (as Jacques Chailley has called it) of the "modern" period; between the unbarred music of the Renaissance (or the sporadically barred music of the dawning Baroque) and the regular ("isochronous") barring of later music. As with the key-signature, one can claim that the music *per se* of Charpentier's piece is more modern than its time-signatures or, to put it another way, that the theoretical implications of the signatures are contradicted by the music.

The signature ₵ 3/2 with which *Alma Redemptoris Mater* begins is an inheritance from the proportional notation of the Renaissance, in which it signified *sesquialtera*, a proportion in which three semibreves are theoretically equal to two under the normal signature of ₵, *proportio dupla*. Here, however, the older meaning does not apply; the music is strictly metrical (and isochronously barred, save at one point) and the time-signature merely summarizes the meter: three minims to the measure, with the minim being the unit of beat.[4] True *sesquialtera* occurs at the one point in the work *not* isochronously barred (measures 27-28 of the edition), where three successive semibreves appear (the manuscript's use of blackened notes here will be discussed shortly), forming a six-beat unit divided 2 + 2 + 2, as opposed to the preceding and succeeding two-measure six-beat units divided 3 + 3.[5] This is the favorite *use* of *sesquialtera* by Baroque-era composers: not, as with Renaissance masters, a subtle proportional change effecting a slight alteration of tempo or permitting intricate cross-rhythms (with other voices not in *sesquialtera*) but a brief and brusque shift of metrical

gears, in *hemiola*,[6] from one triple meter to another—here from 3/2 to 3/1 (equivalent shifts are commonly made also from 3/4 to 3/2 and from 3/8 to 3/4). Measures 28-30 show the typical Baroque-era *placement* of such hemiolic shifts—at a cadence—although they can occur anywhere in triple meters, particularly in dances like the *menuet* and *passepied*.

Charpentier's use of ₵ 3/2, an old proportional sign, raises a question as to the relationship between its note-values and those of the cadential passages, with the signature ₵, of measures 7-8 and 15-16. If ₵ 3/2 were indeed *sesquialtera*, then ₵ 3/2 ♩♩♩ would equal ₵ ♩♩, and these cadences would have built-in ritardandi. This is an attractive idea, but probably untrue. More likely is the equation ₵ 3/2 ♩ = ₵ ♩, as specified by Henri Louis Choquel in his *La Musique rendue sensible par la méchanique* . . . (Paris, 1759), in a discussion of Lully's style.[7] (Otherwise, one might expect Charpentier to have similarly broadened the even more conclusive cadences at measures 41-42 and 97-98). On the other hand, there are two signatures juxtaposed often by Charpentier (and many other French composers of his time) with a strictly proportional relationship: ₵ and C. The equation is ₵ ♩ = C ♩. This relationship is common in the recitatives of Lullian *tragédies lyriques* and later French cantatas. But it is observed by Charpentier also in sacred works, and not just in recitative passages. One of his Magnificats, for example (VIII, 34ff),[8] for four solo voices and basso continuo, begins as in Ex. 1-a. Later, he wrote an instrumental prelude for the work, basing it on the opening vocal theme; this he notated not in C but in ₵ (Ex. 1-b), and clearly ₵ ♩ = C ♩, since the brief prelude must certainly be in the same tempo as the canticle's opening.

A similar proportion obtains between 2 and C meters in Charpentier's music, as in Lully's: 2 ♩ = C ♩.[9] This suggests that, so far as general tempo-implications go, 2 = ₵ —a matter of inter-

Ex. 1
a. Canticum B.V.M. (VIII, 34), mm. 1–3 (b.c. omitted).

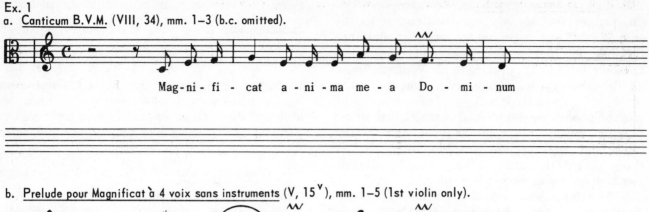

Mag - ni - fi - cat   a - ni -ma me - a   Do - mi - num

b. Prelude pour Magnificat à 4 voix sans instruments (V, 15ᵛ), mm. 1–5 (1st violin only).

est to us in view of measures 43-63 of *Alma Redemptoris Mater*, in **2** meter.[10] Why then did Charpentier bother to use the two different signatures? I believe it can be argued that when ₵ is the basic meter of a passage (not just a cadential shift from triple meter as here in measures 7-8 and 15-16) it is intended to signify a measure of four fast beats, whereas **2** signifies a measure of two slow beats. In the Gloria of his *Missa Assumpta est Maria* (XXVII, 1-14ᵛ), for instance, Charpentier's alternation of ₵ and **2** meters seems to aim at this differentiation, the ₵-meter passages (in a stomping quadruple) being marked "gai" (fast) and the **2**-meter passage (clearly duple) marked "lent" (Ex. 2). In other works, when a verbal tempo indication appears together with ₵ meter, it is often marked "gai," while with **2** meter we find "à 2 temps graves" or "lentement," as well as "lent." Étienne Loulié seems to confirm this interpretation of ₵ meter when he gives priority, in his explanation of it, to a four-beat measure (although not excluding a duple reading): "On se sert du C barré [₵] pour le signe de la mesure à quatre temps vites, ou deux temps lents. . . ."[11]

The note-shapes. The passages in ₵**3⁄2** meter include two kinds of note-shapes meriting discussion. Like other aspects of the notation that we have observed, these too are *retardataires* and were not to outlive Charpentier by long; they are not,

however, unique to his music and are frequently found in the scores of other seventeenth-century composers, especially French and Italian. These are the "white eighths" (and "sixteenths"), and the blackened semibreves.

The "croches blanches" seem to have originated in France a century and a half before Charpentier: they were introduced by Pierre Attaingnant in his first publications of keyboard music. Although Attaingnant used the conventional blackened minim (♩) to represent a semiminim in his publications of vocal music, in his keyboard prints he also represented it by a white minim with a flag (♪); similarly, the fusa was given as a white minim with two flags (♫).[12] This notational idiosyncrasy spread to Italy by the seventeenth century: we find it in manuscripts and published music by such composers as Monteverdi, D. Mazzocchi, and Carissimi.[13] It was maintained, especially in France, until the eighteenth century: a well-known example of its use is in François Couperin's suite "Les Fastes de la grande et ancienne mxnxstrxndxsx," in his *Second Livre de clavecin* of 1717. The notational device had no esoteric meaning; as Carissimi explains it (if indeed it was Carissimi who authored the German treatise published under his name): "Die weisse Noten aber Minime, so fern sie mit einem Schweiss gesehen werden [♪], so kommen sie in der Geltung und allem mit den semiminimis [♩] überein."[14] Charpentier always uses *croches blanches* when he

Ex. 2. <u>Missa Assumpta est Maria</u>, Gloria, mm. 23–40 (1st soprano and b.c. parts only).

writes in ₵ $\frac{3}{2}$ meter, seldom when he writes in sim-ple $\frac{3}{2}$; I cannot explain this difference in his no-tation of the two.

The blackened semibreves (measures 27-28 and 79-80 of the edition) are used, as has been suggested above, to indicate hemiola. The note-values are the same as if the notes were not blackened, as Loulié explains: "S'il se rencontre des notes noires dans le Triple blanc, elles valent autant que si elles étaient blanches."[15] In measures 79-80, only the upper voice is in hemiola—in that voice, these two measures should be felt as a single one in $\frac{3}{1}$, otherwise the text will come out misaccented—and it alone is written by Charpentier in blackened notes (with the second semibreve squarely astride the bar line). In the original manuscript passage corresponding to measures 27-28 of the edition, there is no bar line; the three semibreves fill a single "measure" effectively in $\frac{3}{1}$.

But, unconsciously acknowledging the basically isochronous meter of his music, when Charpentier tallies up the length of the work (see his figure "98" at the end of the manuscript) he counts the blackened-note passage as two measures.

The foregoing discussion has touched on a few interesting aspects of notation in Charpentier's *Alma Redemptoris Mater*. Their implications for a modern edition of the work might be summarized as follows:

1. A single flat as a key-signature for a composition in B-flat major was recognized as an anachronism, "une erreur considérable," even within Charpentier's lifetime. The signature should have two flats.

2. The tempo relationships—i.e., the relationships of note-values—among the work's three time-signatures can be adduced. They should be indicated editorially (see measures 6-7, 8-9, and elsewhere). The duple character of the manuscript's **2** meter should be affirmed (see measure 43).

3. The time-signature ₵ $\frac{3}{2}$, a legacy of Renaissance proportional notation, had lost its meaning as such by the mid-seventeenth century, and its notation in *croches blanches* was simply a conventionally idiosyncratic substitute for "normal" notation. The signature should be a simple $\frac{3}{2}$ and the notation normalized. The blackened semibreves, another holdover from mensural notation, should also be normalized; on the other hand, their signaling of a hemiolic shift of real meter is important musically and valuable to the performer, and the edition should reflect this (see the editorial brackets above the staff in measures 27-28 and 79-80).

* * *

A few other aspects of the music of *Alma Redemptoris Mater* invite some citation, and their implications for a modern edition may be suggested very briefly.

The medium. The work is probably for two solo voices, not for chorus. Charpentier's mention-ing "deux hautes contres" (and not, for example, "deux parties d'haute contre") in a note preceding the music is one basis for this assumption. Another is that in its general dimensions and its lack of indications for exploiting the choral medium that are typical of Charpentier's works for chorus—shifts from full choir (*tous* or *grand choeur*) to *petit choeur* of soloists, or alternation and combination of half-choirs—*Alma Redemptoris Mater* seems quite clearly to belong to the category of the *petit motet* for solo voices. The basso continuo's instrumentation is not specified here, but in other *petits motets* Charpentier almost always indicates "orgue" (when he indicates any instrument at all), without an additional melodic bass instrument. Thus it would be appropriate in a modern edition to call for two sopranos and organ.

The key. Not clear in the facsimile is that Charpentier's original title was simply "Alma redem." At another time he added to it, and the final result may be translated "The following Alma Redem[ptoris Mater] can be sung by two counter-tenors by transposing the basso continuo a [whole-]tone higher." I have elsewhere published the list of keys and their corresponding "affects" that Charpentier once set out for a royal pupil.[16] That list suggests that Charpentier's choice of key for a work was determined by the particular affect appropriate to the text he was setting. Here, however, we see him as a practical musician, ready to have this work in B-flat major ("magnificent and joyous" is his characterization of that key) transposed to C major ("gay and warlike") if, instead of two sopranos, only two countertenors are at hand. The implication for an editor should be clear: there is no reason not to transpose if there is an advantage to doing so. In the present work, because of the high tessitura of the upper soprano part a sweeter-sounding performance (and "sweet" is the way I would characterize this music) may be possible by transposing the piece down by a half-step to A major (according to Charpentier a "joyous and pastoral" key),[17] although in the accompanying edition, for ease in comparing it with the facsimile of the original, it has been left in B-flat.

The ornaments. In the manuscript, ornaments are indicated (by the single sign $\sim\!\!\!\sim$) four times in the upper soprano part, four times in the lower. All these indications occur within the first third of the composition. Not to add others—specifically, more of the short trills that seem appropriate at the places already indicated by the composer—would be to leave the work out of balance indeed. Thus, more should be added, following the hints given by Charpentier's sporadic ornamentation itself, at cadences and at other points where brief ornaments will highlight the proper accentuation of the text (as they already do, at Charpentier's hands, in measures 28, 30, 31, 34, and 35). No more precise "rules" can be adduced for such additions; one can only trust (as in fact French treatises emphasize) *le bon goût*.

Another type of "ornamentation" in French music of the Baroque era, a rhythmic one, is inequality (in performance) of notes written equal (in the music): *notes inégales*. Whether in the present work the evenly-written scale passages in short notes in measures 20-21, 25-26, 60-63, and 88-89 should be made uneven (long-short) is an unavoidable question. It is also perhaps unanswerable. Not only does a controversy still rage as to the nature and proper application of *notes inégales*, but—especially as regards Charpentier—the question is moot since not once, in all the thousands of measures of his more-than-500 works in autograph manuscripts, does he suggest *notes inégales*.[18]

The figuration and realization. Charpentier's figuration is comparatively complete in the present manuscript; few harmonic uncertainties exist, and it would seem tautological to add more figures. Since the voice-parts are definitely in the foreground all the time, and since there is no instrumental prelude, ritornel, or epilogue, a continuo realization of elemental simplicity would seem appropriate. And in view of the diminutive resources demanded, it can best be kept very light, with very few doublings of chord tones (and as few as possible of the voice-parts).

* * *

NOTES

1. For a slightly more detailed discussion of this matter, see my study, "Marc-Antoine Charpentier and the Comédie-Française," *Journal of the American Musicological Society*, XXIV (1971), 255-81.

2. *Ibid.*, note 3.

3. M[onsieur?] de Saint-Lambert, *Nouveau Traité de l'accompagnement du clavecin, de l'orgue, et des autres instruments* (Paris: Christophe Ballard, 1707).

4. At about the same time that Charpentier composed *Alma Redemptoris Mater*, time-signatures were explained for the first time as having precisely this meaning—by Giovanni Maria Bononcini, in his *Musico prattico...* (Bologna, 1673).

5. The uppermost voice at the point in the original manuscript corresponding to measures 79-80 of the edition is similarly notated.

6. As Morley puts it, "Hemiolia doth signify that which the Latins term Sesquipla or Sesquialtera, but the good monks... gave it that name of Hemiolia for lack of

another." See Thomas Morley, *A Plain and Easy Introduction to Practical Music*, ed. R. Alec Harmon (London: J. M. Dent & Sons, 1952), p. 52.

7. Cited in Eugène Borrel, "L'Interprétation de l'ancien récitatif français," *Revue de musicologie*, XII (1931), 13-21.

8. Works in Charpentier's "Mélanges autographes" will be referred to simply by volume and page numbers.

9. Compare, for example, the beginning of the dramatic motet *Pestis Mediolanensis* (III, 120) with a prelude written later for it (XVII, 41ᵛ) which is, like the Magnificat prelude just cited, based on the same theme.

10. Ample evidence is to be found elsewhere in Charpentier's works to confirm this equation. See, for example, a *Motet pour les trépassés* (I, 27), which has an instrumental prelude (in **2**) based on the same music as the beginning of the motet proper (in **₵**); see also two settings of the *Litanies de la Vierge* (Litaniae Lauretanae) in which tempo-equivalence between the two meters is similarly demonstrated (XI, 1-4 and XXII, 88ᵛ-91).

11. *Eléments ou principes de musique...* (Paris: Christophe Ballard, 1696), pp. 60-61. But one cannot argue very strongly on this point: in another Mass (X, 23-51), at exactly the same moment in the Gloria, and with a very similar rhythmic and affective differentiation between "Laudamus te" and "Adoramus te," Charpentier reverses the order of the two signatures.

12. See the introduction to Albert Seay's edition of Pierre Attaingnant, *Transcriptions of Chansons for Keyboard* (Corpus Mensurabilis Musicae, 20) (n.p.: American Institute of Musicology, 1961), p. 11. Willi Apel, *The Notation of Polyphonic Music 900-1600* (5th ed.; Cambridge, Mass.: Medieval Academy of America, 1953), p. 7 gives a facsimile from Attaingnant's *Quatorze Gaillardes...* (Paris, 1530) which shows these note-shapes.

13. See, for example, the following: Giacomo Carissimi, *Six Solo Cantatas*, ed. Gloria Rose (London: Faber Music Limited, 1969), p. 86 (commentary on *Bel tempo per me se n'andò*); Domenico Mazzocchi, *La Catena d'Adone* (Venice, 1626; repr. Bologna, Forni Editore, [1969]), p. 116; Claudio Monteverdi, *L'Incoronazione di Poppea* (Venice, Bibl. Marcia, Codice Contarini, Cl. 4, No. 439, coll. 9963; facs. ed. Bologna: Forni Editore, [1969]), solo of Fortuna in the Prologue.

14. *Ars Cantandi; das ist: richtiger und ausführlicher Weg die Jugend aus dem rechten Grund in der Sing-Kunst zu unterrichten...* (Augsburg: Jacob Koppmayer, 1693), p. 12.

15. *Eléments ou principes*, p. 61. Carissimi (*Ars Cantandi*, p. 12) says the same thing: "Die ganze schwarze viereck-tichte Noten [▬ and ◆ , in the examples he gives] gelten zwar nicht mehr noch weniger als die weisse in ihrer Form...."

16. "The Latin Oratorios of Marc-Antoine Charpentier," *The Musical Quarterly*, XLI (1955), 41-65.

17. Many French sacred works of the period invite such a downward transposition. This may reflect the pitch of organs in Paris and Versailles—about a whole tone higher, in the 17th century, than $a^1 = 440$. See *Studies in the History of Musical Pitch: Monographs by Alexander J. Ellis and Arthur Mendel* (Amsterdam: Fritz Knuf, 1968), pp. 221, 238.

18. It might be more meaningful to put it the other way: not once does he call for *notes égales*. *Notes inégales* seem to have been so conventional, at least with some composers, that they themselves are almost never mentioned.

Alma Redemptoris Mater

Marc-Antoine Charpentier
ed. by H. Wiley Hitchcock

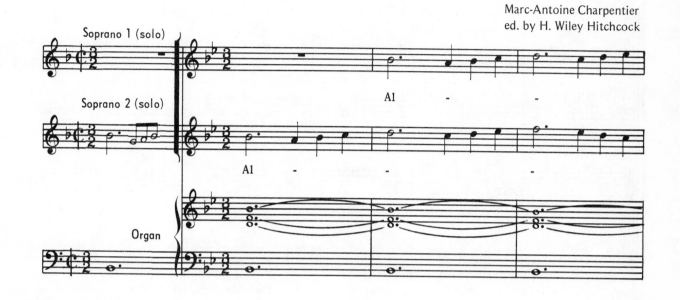

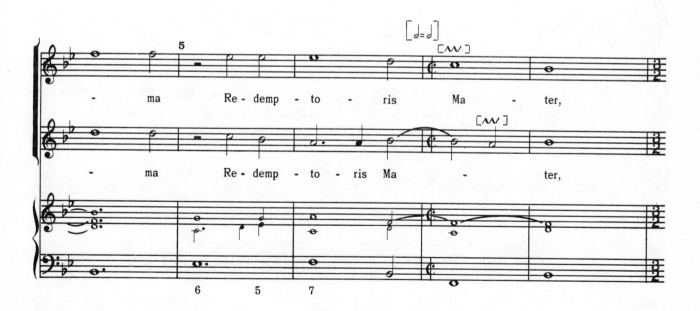

* E♮ in the original.

11

Problems in Editing Harpsichord Music:
Suite in D by Ferdinand Tobias Richter (1649-1711)

C. David Harris
DRAKE UNIVERSITY

Appointed in 1683 to the Hofkapelle of Leopold I, Ferdinand Tobias Richter soon won fame for his keyboard performance, composition, and tutoring. Musicians from north of the Alps visited him in Vienna, and to him, together with Buxtehude, Pachelbel dedicated the *Hexachordum Apollinis*. Among those whom Richter tutored were the Emperor's children, including the Archduke, to be crowned Joseph I in 1705. In the same manuscript containing the *Suite in D*, there is a brief keyboard suite by Richter inscribed to the Archduke; it may be that the Suite in D included here also was written for one of the royal children, for its technical demands do not illustrate the virtuosity ascribed to Richter and found in certain of his other works for keyboard.

The source of the Suite is music manuscript XIV 743 of the Minoritenkonvent in Vienna. Besides the suite for the Archduke, this same manuscript contains one other unpublished suite by Richter and the three suites edited by Hugo Botstiber in *Denkmäler der Tonkunst in Österreich, XIII/ii*.

As is customary in the Austrian keyboard repertoire of the time, the right-hand part of the Suite uses the soprano clef, for which the treble clef has been substituted in the following edition. Certain of the notes have been transferred from one hand's part to the other, and what appear to be errors by the scribe have been amended. A listing of editorial changes appears below.

The chief problem of an edition of this nature, however, concerns the revival of various aspects of performance practice. The manuscript source is nearly devoid of suggestions for performance: only the notes, signatures of key and meter, and infrequent trill signs are provided. Thus the original version is typical of much early

Suite in D by Ferdinand Tobias Richter (Minoritenkonvent, Vienna, Ms xiv, 743). With permission of the Minoritenkonvent.

keyboard music, especially outside France. Moreover, clues pertaining to the performance practices of a composer or school may not appear in exactly contemporary sources and may have to be inferred from slightly earlier or later sources. For example, Gottlieb Muffat's *Componimenti musicali per il cembalo* (c. 1735) is especially valuable, for it contains not only precise signs for various ornaments but also directions for phrasing and articulation. A number of phrasings, markings of articulation, and ornaments have been introduced in the edition that follows. Ornament signs not appearing in the manuscript source are placed within brackets.

Together with considerations of Baroque performance practice, a sense of the kinetic aspects of playing early keyboard instruments will be useful in editing keyboard music of the time. In addition, acquaintance with early keyboard fingerings may be helpful; some suggestions for fingerings based on early patterns are introduced in the Courante of the following Suite.

In several instances, important interpretative decisions will have to be made by the performer. The first of these involves the dotted values of the Entrée, the form and style of which correspond to the French overture. While overdotting is idiomatic in French overture style, the performer should decide the extent of overdotting—whether to doubledot or to overdot with a less precise ratio; whether to overdot the dotted quarter-notes as well as the dotted eighth-notes; and when to apply a silence of articulation between a dotted note and the following short note. These are matters of musicianship; including their solution in an edition would detract from the fundamental appearance of the music and from spontaneity in performance. Moreover, realization of the overdotting may vary according to the instrument being played.

Another decision confronts the performer at measures 35 and 36 of the Entrée and possibly in the final measures of the Allemande and Sarabande as well. In each instance the left hand is to play an interval of a tenth or more. While it will be possible for the right hand to play the upper note of the interval in the Allemande and Sarabande, the texture of the Entrée precludes this solution. Performers who cannot reach the tenths in the Entrée should arpeggiate them. Richter was probably writing for an instrument with a short octave

arrangement in the bass, in which case these intervals would have presented no difficulty. In a typical short octave arrangement, apparent $F\sharp$ sounds D and apparent $G\sharp$ sounds E. Since both $F\sharp$ and $G\sharp$, as well as D and E, are required in the Entrée, however, it seems more likely that Richter was writing for an instrument with a split key short octave in the bass. In this arrangement of keys, the $F\sharp$ and $G\sharp$ keys are split, with half of the $F\sharp$ key tuned to D, the other half to $F\sharp$. Similarly, half of the $G\sharp$ key would be tuned to E, the other half to $G\sharp$. In such an arrangement the two tenths of the Entrée passage would be played like a normal seventh and octave. Harpsichords with this split key short octave do not survive in Vienna, but a number of Italian examples remain. In view of the Imperial court's penchant for all things Italian and the known importation of Italian keyboard instruments during the reign of Leopold, it seems probable that such instruments were known in Vienna during Richter's tenure at the court.

Still another decision for the performer concerns the length of the trills; in any case they should begin on the upper auxiliary and should contain a minimum of four notes. The wedge sign indicating detached notes is introduced in conformance with Baroque practice, in which both the wedge and the vertical dash generally indicated halving of the value of notes marked by them. The comparable modern keyboard articulation would be *portato* touch. The dot indicating *staccato* is introduced in the edition as well, and is intended to signify shorter duration than that of notes marked with the wedge. On the harpsichord, notes on important beats can be accented by holding them slightly longer than the others, even though all are detached.

It remains to cite instances of apparent error in the manuscript, the only known source of this Suite. In the Entrée, the scribe almost certainly misplaced the *alla breve* signature, for in the manuscript source it appears four measures before the end rather than at measure 14, as in the present edition. The Minuet begins with a fifth, *a*, but no third in the middle voice, and the given fifth moves to another fifth in the second measure; the given *a* has been replaced with *f♯* in the edition. Other changes are given in the table on the opposite page.

Entrée

Measure 6, *g* in the tenor voice is given as a plain half note.

        7, the left hand's notes are given as tied half notes.

     12, the tenor voice has nothing after the second beat in the manuscript source; *b* has been supplied.

     16, the treble voice is blurred in the manuscript source; beats 3 and 4 might read *f♯"*.

     38, no quarter rest is given in the tenor part.

     40, a repeat is not indicated here, although the sign for repetition appears at measure 14.

Courante

      3, inner voice, third beat; no quarter rest is given.

     10, treble voice; no dot is given after the half note.

     25, the tied *f♯* has been supplied.

First and second endings are not indicated for either section in the manuscript source; the first section closes with the A-major chord in half notes followed by the repeat sign. The second section closes as in the second ending of the edition, but a repeat is indicated.

Minuet

First and second endings are not numbered but are tied in the manuscript source.

     18, the half note appearing in the middle voice is dotted.

Bourrée

     16, no rests are indicated for the fourth beat.

Gigue

     12, the chord on beat 4 is given in dotted quarter notes.

     24, right hand; only the treble voice is given.

Suite in D

Entrée

Ferdinand Tobias Richter
ed. by C. David Harris

Allemande

Courante

Minuet

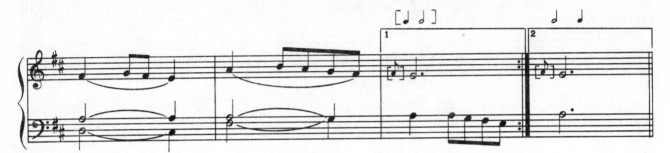

Sarabande

Bourrée

Gigue

12

A Realization by J.C. Heck:
an *Affettuoso di molto*
by Johann Joachim Quantz (1697-1773)

EDWARD R. REILLY
VASSAR COLLEGE

The performance of music of the Baroque period, and of the *galant* era that succeeded it, requires the resolution of many special problems connected with tempo, articulation, ornamentation, and dynamics. Yet the most common task that faces performers and editors of works from these times is the realization of basso continuo parts. The realization presented here of an *Affettuoso di molto* by J. J. Quantz (1697-1773) draws attention to a question associated with continuo practice in the period from about 1725-1780: to what degree did the keyboard player concern himself with dynamic nuance in the realization of his accompaniments? Modern studies discuss some aspects of the dynamics of continuo performance, but the subtler forms of gradation and dynamic stress are often passed over. That at least some eighteenth-century musicians were not indifferent to these matters is underlined by the fact that the realization offered here is the work of a younger contemporary of Quantz, Johann Casper Heck (b. 1740), rather than that of a modern editor.

After a period of reaction to the excesses of some nineteenth-century continuo "elaborations," scholars have recently shown a renewed interest in the varied methods of realization indicated in seventeenth- and eighteenth-century sources. Special attention has been directed to the dynamic and sonorous contrasts between four-part and full-voiced realizations.[1] Quantz's awareness of such contrasts is obvious from the section "Of the Keyboard Player in Particular" in his treatise on the flute (1752),[2] and it is in this work that the principles underlying Heck's later realization are clearly stated for the first time. Much of Quantz's discussion of keyboard accompaniment is taken up with the description of musical situations in which the performer may depart from the normal rules of four-part realization. The closely-related subject of dynamics receives equally careful consideration. The instrument used, the type of composition, the balance between the keyboard and other instrumentalists or singers, the position of the ensemble in the hall or room, and numerous other points are shown to have a significant bearing upon the kind of accompaniment to be used, especially with regard to the appropriate number of parts and the sharpness of the attack of the performer. Quick shifts between few parts and many are accepted as normal. But Quantz also extends his discussion beyond the notion of simple contrasts between soft and loud passages. He indicates that dissonances inherently require additional stress in performance through a more forceful touch and an increase in the number of parts, and that "if several dissonances are resolved into dissonances, you must also allow the expression gradually to swell and diminish by strengthening the tone and increasing the number of parts."[3] He goes on to suggest that different dynamic weights are implicit in several clearly defined categories of dissonances. To illustrate his practice he offers the present *Affettuoso*—in effect a sonata slow movement—in unrealized form, with an exceptional profusion of dynamic markings to suggest the various shadings that he intended[4] (see the facsimile). In his text he adds the important qualification that the contrasts between the different dynamic levels are not to be too strong.

F. T. Arnold, in his *The Art of Accompaniment from a Thorough-Bass*, reviews Quantz's discussion of keyboard accompaniment in some detail, and reproduces the present movement in its original form. He also draws attention to C. P. E. Bach's general agreement with Quantz in the matter of stressing dissonances, and Bach's reserva-

Facsimile of J. J. Quantz's Affettuoso di molto, from his *Versuch einer Anweisung die Flöte traversiere zu spielen* (Berlin, 1752). Courtesy of the Library of Congress, Washington, D. C.

tions about carrying this notion to the point of a schematic classification of dissonant chords such as that provided by Quantz.[5] To my knowledge, however, no example of an eighteenth-century realization embodying this type of dynamic shading has been cited in the modern literature on thorough-bass. Thus Heck's handling of the piece is of some importance in confirming that Quantz's general approach was not peculiar to himself, and in indicating precisely how an accompanist might achieve these dynamic nuances. The fact that Heck's work did not appear in print until the 1760s is also a useful reminder of the persistence of the traditions of continuo playing into the Classic period.[6]

Heck's realization of the continuo of the *Affettuoso* movement appeared in his *The Art of Playing Thorough Bass* (c. 1767; later editions 1793 and c. 1795),[7] where it follows more customary realizations of four movements from Corelli's trio sonatas.[8] Heck, like Quantz, presents the *Affettuoso* to exemplify an especially refined style of accompaniment in which dissonances may be underlined either individually or successively. Heck does not discuss or rigidly adhere to Quantz's graduated classification of dissonances. He also, rather curiously, omits all but one of the original dynamic markings (which are restored in the present edition). Yet there can be no question that he is illustrating the central principle put forward by Quantz. The approach is relatively simple. The basic harmonization is in three parts. Some triads preceding dissonances, however, and most dissonant chords are realized in four parts. Both are thus automatically given somewhat more weight. To intensify certain dissonant chords still more, and to reinforce the deceptive cadence in measure 36, the bass is doubled at the lower octave. Quantz's own discussion of his example indicates that he might have gone somewhat further in left-hand doubling of the consonant notes of his stronger seventh chords. Quantz also suggests the introduction of rapid upward arpeggiation for the strongest dissonances, and the use of the upper manual of a two-manual harpsichord for pianissimo passages.[9] Since this style of accompaniment reflects an interest in the kind of dynamic gradation that ultimately led to the replacement of the harpsichord by the pianoforte, it is not surprising that Quantz already singles out the latter instrument as one on which "everything required may be accomplished with the greatest convenience."[10] Heck, on the other hand, still prefers the harpsichord for the accompaniment of solos.[11]

In his harmonization of the bass Heck does not hesitate to write parallel octaves with the solo part, as long as the parallels are kept in the inner voices of the accompaniment (see, for example, measures 9-10). In general he keeps the upper voice of the realization below the solo line, but does not shun occasional unisons, especially when the flute part descends into the lower register (see, for example, measure 41).

A realization of this sort raises several questions. How early was this practice used? How widespread was it? And in what types of composition was it appropriate? Quantz's discussion of accompaniment dates from 1752, but all of the evidence connected with Quantz's work as a performer and composer indicates that his style was fully formed by the 1730s at the latest, and there is no reason to assume that his views on accompaniment form an exception. The specific recommendation of the keyboard section of Quantz's treatise by Marpurg (who reprinted it in 1763),[12] G. M. Telemann, and C. G. Schröter,[13] suggests that the approach of Quantz (and Heck) was not uncommon, and for experienced and sensitive players represented an accepted alternative to straightforward four-part realization. While dynamic shading was well known in connection with solo vocal and instrumental parts in much earlier times, the situation with regard to continuo realization is less clear in the seventeenth and early eighteenth centuries. I have discovered no unequivocal description or illustration of a comparable continuo practice in the theoretical works of these times. Among later sources, Türk's *Klavierschule* of 1789 shows that the principle of stressing dissonances survived in pianoforte performance in the Classic period.[14]

The nature of the practice illustrated by Heck clearly limits the types of works in which such shading can be used. Only in compositions in a moderate to very slow tempo would so many shifts in the number of parts be practicable. And only in compositions, instrumental or vocal, with a very small complement of performers would these subtle gradations be perceptible. Performance in a small chamber rather than in a large hall or theater is also implicit. Whether the practice has any national stylistic associations is still uncertain. If this example may be taken as typical, an Italian background is clearly present.

While the purpose of the present example is to illustrate one particular type of realization, the editor of Baroque and *galant* music must be equally aware of other possibilities. Different types of four-part, embellished, or full-voiced accompaniments are appropriate in different works, depending upon their style and the period in which they were written. But in continuo realization, as in such matters as ornamentation and phrasing, the editor must also consider carefully to what extent he is going to leave the modern performer with the freedom of his eighteenth-century counterpart, and to what degree he is going to limit that freedom by spelling out only one of several possible alternatives. The editor's response to this basic question will affect every aspect of his work. Some freedom may be preserved for the performer in continuo parts by including the original bass figures (if there are any), thus allowing him to modify the editorial realization at will. Yet no rigid editorial procedure is satisfactory. A tempo marking in a work from about 1745, for example, may be relatively clear to a modern player, while the use of the term *presto* or *largo* in 1675 may require a special explanation. In Quantz's case, a fairly specific indication of his notion of the tempo of the present movement may be gained from the system of tempo classification outlined in his treatise,[15] but the possibility of indicating tempi with the same degree of precision in many other works of this time is more remote.

Ornamentation also poses complex problems. Again the editor must choose between a specific interpretation for the performer (notated realizations of appoggiaturas and trills, written out variations of the melodic line where they are appropriate) and general directions that indicate alternatives from which the performer may choose or the sources from which he may learn these alternatives. Although the latter approach is in some respects more risky, it is the one most favored today—and in my opinion rightly so. Some performers are unwilling to accept the obligations imposed by the freedom to make their own decisions, but those who do have a fuller opportunity to recover the freshness and spontaneity of the more improvisatory approach of the eighteenth century. Following Quantz's instructions,[16] an editor could write out a number of variations in the solo part of this movement. In performance, however, the resulting line will rarely sound as if it is actually improvised. Through direct study of Quantz's examples of free variations, on the other hand, some performers can develop a genuine improvisational ability. Then as now, "those who lack this skill will always do better to prefer the invention of the composer to their own fancies."[17]

In the matter of the smaller embellishments, unless granted the special privilege of a lengthy introduction or extensive footnotes, the editor is rarely in a position to describe how all of the appoggiaturas, mordents, trills, and turns might be interpreted. In this *Affettuoso* some basic generalizations could be offered in connection with the handling of the trills. Normally the trills would begin with the upper auxiliary to the principal note (notated in measure 5, assumed elsewhere), unless the preceding note in the melody is already an upper or lower neighbour that is slurred to the main note (as in measures 13, 25, etc.). In this example this initial appoggiatura should not be lengthened in most cases, because of the dissonant harmonic situations in which the trills appear (see measures 4, 10, 12).[18] Most of the trills should be played evenly, not too quickly, and with a termination. Having reviewed these and other rules from Quantz's treatise,[19] however, few perceptive performers will fail to realize that they can be interpreted in a variety of ways, and that a number of situations appear in the piece that are not entirely covered by such directions. The notated appoggiaturas in measures 28 and 33 are less problematic, since both fall into Quantz's category of "passing" appoggiaturas. Hence they are played before the beat or its subdivision.[20] Yet other performers of the same period may well have played them quickly in the time of the principal notes. Additional appoggiaturas, trills, or mordents, might also have been added as elements of improvised variations.

The interpretation of the dynamics and ornamentation of this work will in turn obviously affect phrasing and articulation. In exploring all of the rich variety of possibilities that present themselves in connection with each aspect of performance, both the editor and the player ultimately must make subjective decisions about what seems the most appropriate and effective solution of a specific problem. The editor's role, in my opinion, must be to guide the player, by offering alternatives and their historical sources, rather than to impose a specific interpretation upon him. Only when the performer's freedom is restored to him can he learn to use and to enjoy it.

NOTES

1. See especially G. J. Buelow, *Thorough-Bass Accompaniment according to Johann David Heinichen* (Berkeley: University of California Press, 1966).

2. J. J. Quantz, *On Playing the Flute*, trans. E. R. Reilly (New York: The Free Press, 1966), pp. 250-265.

3. *Ibid.*, p. 258.

4. *Ibid.*, p. 257.

5. F. T. Arnold, *The Art of Accompaniment from a Thorough-Bass* (London: Oxford University Press, 1931), I, pp. 407-414.

6. Breitkopf's catalogues advertise numerous works with continuo parts into the 1780s.

7. Virtually nothing is known about Heck except that he was a German immigrant to England, where several of his instructional works were published in the late 1760s and 1770s. The *Affettuoso* appears on pp. 96-97 of the first edition of *The Art of Playing Thorough Bass* (London: John Welcker). The later editions of the volume were issued in London by John Preston. Although the first edition of the treatise has been previously dated c. 1777, a Welcker catalogue of 1767 shows that the work had appeared at least by that time.

8. *Ibid.*, pp. 94-96. Quantz's piece is followed by an excerpt "From a Passione Compos'd by Graun," pp. 98-99.

9. Quantz, *op. cit.*, p. 259.

10. *Ibid.*

11. Heck, *op. cit.*, p. 92.

12. It appeared in part 3 of Marpurg's *Clavierstücke mit einem practischen Unterricht für Anfänger und Geübter* (Berlin: Haude und Spener).

13. Arnold, *op. cit.*, I, pp. 291-292, 299.

14. D. G. Türk, *Klavierschule* (Leipzig: Schwickert, 1789), pp. 350-351.

15. Quantz, *op. cit.*, pp. 283-292.

16. *Ibid.*, pp. 136-161, 169-172.

17. *Ibid.*, p. 139.

18. On this particular point, see Quantz, *ibid.*, p. 96.

19. *Ibid.*, pp. 100-108.

20. *Ibid.*, pp. 93-94, 228.

Affetuoso di molto

Johann Joachim Quantz
Realization by J.C. Heck
ed. by Edward R. Reilly

13

TEMA, Opus 13
Robert Alexander Schumann (1810-1856)

JOHN L. KOLLEN

THE UNIVERSITY OF MICHIGAN

"The life of every man . . . it were good to remember, is a Poem."
—Thomas Carlyle, *Count Cagliostro*[1]

The interest in the mysterious effects of nature and magic on the life of man which pervaded the climate of German literature and music during the time of Robert Schumann not only stimulated but also contributed to the genius of his complex creative nature.[2] Although there is evidence that he studied Marpurg's *Abhandlung von der Fuge*, it was primarily the aesthetic theories of the "Affects" as well as "Embellishment" in the treatises of Quantz and C.P.E. Bach which chiefly concerned him. Since Schumann was well aware of his contemporaries, he was somewhat influenced by Clementi, Cramer, Field (debatable), Paganini, Moscheles, and Chopin. Furthermore, beyond his interest in Weber's pianoforte works, he captured his keen sense of orchestral color and character delineation, transferring it to the piano's expanded resources for sonority as foreseen by Beethoven. Having had the impulse to compose music from the age of seven, Schumann did earnestly seek instruction in theory, composition, and keyboard technics, but despite his desire for technical knowledge, he enjoyed only short periods of expert guidance. Though his historical viewpoint on music was limited, his superb power of critical investigation was not, and it led him in his own way to learn most from: J.S. Bach, to him the Source; Beethoven, to him the Originator of the Romantic movement; and Schubert, to him the Spirit of the Dance in the purity of pianistic sonorities and subtle harmonic deflections. Moreover, it is fortunate that he did possess a natural ability to transmute his own creative poetic tendencies into music.

Schumann's growth to maturity in musical composition was astonishingly rapid and reached an early *high level* of creative activity in compositions for the piano in 1832 with the masterly second version of the *Toccata*, and in 1833 the thematically loosely-related first and third movements of the *G minor Sonata*. The following year, during which the *Neue Zeitschrift für Musik* was established, he commenced two major works of contrasting character: the mask, *Carnaval, Scènes mignonnes sur quatre notes* (with its symbolic pseudo neumes headed "Sphinx"), and the metaphysical *Etudes Symphoniques*. His choice of inscription for each of these as published in 1837 is significant. Upon reflection, that for *Carnaval*, Opus 9, is self-explanatory. For the *Symphonic Studies*, Opus 13, one must search further.

During the two years partially devoted to composition of the *Studies*, in the *Neue Zeitschrift für Musik* Schumann militantly attacked the prevailing popular digital style of keyboard display which often exploited superficial variations on familiar airs. But from the very inception of the journal he wrote of "Etude" as being a "Study" in the highest sense of the word, and that it should demand "mastery of a single problem, be it in Technic, Rhythm, Expression, or Performance." Leon Plantinga brings strong evidence to bear that Schumann thought of each *Partita* in *Part I* of Bach's *Clavier-Übung* as a series of "études" and that he also spoke of the *Allemande* of the *B-flat Partita* as an "exercise."[3] Though the foreshortened theme of the *Symphonic Studies* is not to be com-

PLATE 1

R. Schumann, the Theme, Opus 13. Tob. Haslinger (Wien), 1837.

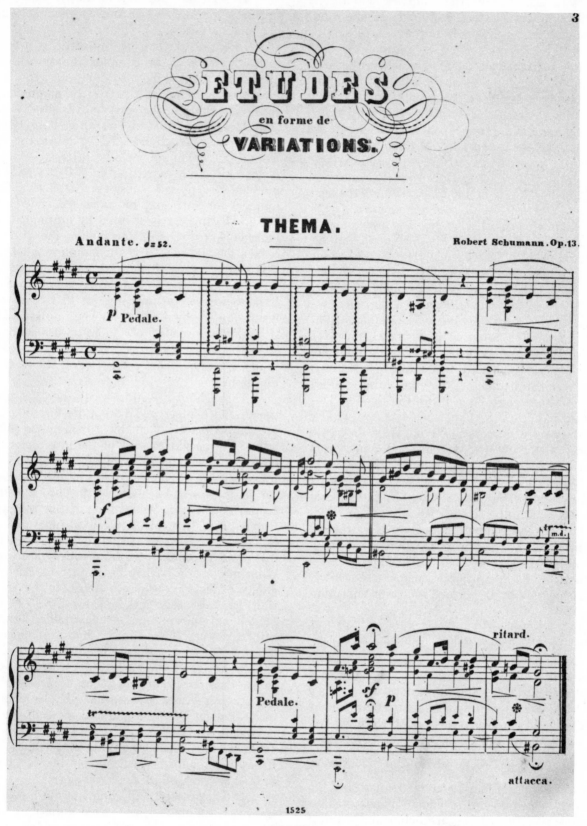

PLATE 2

R. Schumann, the Revised Theme, Opus 13. Schuberth & Comp. (Hamburg, Leipsig, New York) 1852.

pared with the *Aria* of the *Goldberg Variations (Part IV)*, in structuring it Schumann did find nourishment in such roots from the past. It is especially noteworthy that roughly midway through the whole plan of Opus 13 (Etude VII in the first edition, and Variation VI in the second) one finds a sole study entirely in the tonality of E major which indicates the closure of the first part. Both editions then have a fresh opening (though not so indicated) for the second part, a grandiose *Character Piece* ("sempre marcatissimo") based on the dotted-note rhythm of an *Ouverture*. It is also notable that in *Part III* of the *Clavier-Übung* the harmonies of *Duetto IV* anticipate Schumann's.

Schumann originally intended to give Opus 13 the title "Zwölf Davidsbündler Etüden" but he changed this to "Etüden im Orchester Character von Florestan und Eusebius" before he finally settled, in the first imprint (1837), on *XII ETUDES SYMPHONIQUES pour le Pianoforte.*[4] He had inherited the conception of the Davidsbund from Hoffmann and the potential orchestral character of sonorities in the pianoforte from Beethoven. The ear for playing the sounds of Schumann's works is far different from that for playing those of Chopin's. In the second issue (1852), after Mendelssohn had published *17 Variations sérieuses* (1841), he ambiguously compromised between that title ("Etudes") and the first sketches and manuscripts ("Variations"), with the result: *ETUDES en forme de VARIATIONS*. Also, feeling that for Etudes III (Vivace) and IX (Presto possibile), "Variation" was too loose a term, he retained that of "Etude." In each edition the graphic delineation is extremely clear because of Schumann's *restraint* in outlining performance directions. The presentation is, therefore, not for the eyes of philistines. Consequently, the art of recreative performance remains uninhibited.

The edition of 1852, at the close of the Theme into E major, contains the syncopated upbeat rhythmic motif, a detail which gives its two immediately following appearances the character of reminiscence, thus smoothing out and giving a sense of longer continuity. It also contains for the first phrase of the second section a revision of slurring. In both editions, following the open-ended close on the $\frac{6}{4}$ chord threshold, the reduction in texture to quartet-like style is dramatically enhanced by the first use of equally large notes for each voice. Most baffling are Schumann's use of the *alla breve* in the first edition, and in *both*, his choice of the dubious *slurrings*.

To scan the subtleties of motivic detail in the finished model of the Theme, as Alban Berg did in his famous essay on "Träumerei,"[5] would be to show a foreshadowing of the artful constructive technics in that more complex variation. But for our purpose it is enough to point out a fundamental example. Schumann strikes the mood at once. In broad rhythm the bass moves downward in C-sharp minor, I-IV-I. The three-note melodic motif spans a sixth by striding down the chord from $c^{\sharp 2}$. Then the melody, after stretching directly up another sixth from $c^{\sharp 1}$, where it is momentarily poised, subsides conjunctly. At the moment of suspense, on what *seems* to be the strong IV, the ear is arrested by movement of an inner voice to b-sharp, thus making the tritone. At once a metamorphosis in the harmony takes place. The chord seems to expand, and then, with the step-wise lowering in the given melody, to contract, before a startling and, for that time, daring resolution of the dissonance. The resolved suspension blurs the realism of a more traditional dotted-note rhythmic figure. A living compounded harmony breathes. The character of the theme is established.

Throughout the entire work the signs for the use of the damper pedal are spare, pertinent, and accurately placed. Generally its tread is suitably left to the imaginative ear of the interpreter. Elsewhere, it is combined with staccato touch, added for short enhancements of sonority in rhythm, or for long bass notes marked: "Tenuto il Pedale"; "quasi Pedale"; or "Marcato il Thema sempre col Pedale." The sign for its release is sometimes given only *alone*, or occasionally *delayed* to indicate the joining of two phrases. Infrequently, fingerings are given—never for facility but rather to clarify the choice of legato or staccato touch. In the first edition "ten" is used. This is changed to "∧" in the second but the meaning remains. Stem directions of notes clearly show the continuity of inner lines or, when desired, special voicing for the color of chosen notes within a chord. Customarily, directions such as "ritardando" or "crescendo" are spaced with dashes between the syllables. Thus one reads flowingly through the full extent of the gradual change to the "do." A rare exception does occur in the second edition. This comes either from an error in the plate, or represents a decline in taste which has increased ever since.

It is probable that Schumann did not include the five posthumously published Variations,[6] all of which are of lyrical beauty, because he felt that the superb Etude Variation in G$^{\sharp}$ minor was sufficient

PLATE 3

R. Schumann, holograph of the original construction of the Theme, Opus 13.[7] This primary source, marked *alla breve*, reveals the composer's innermost thinking which is concealed in his polished publications. To be noted are: the conventional enclosed bisectional form with repetitions at the feminine endings, the overly-elaborate melody in the consequent clause of the first period, genuine slurrings, pedal indications, dynamics with gradations of sound, the mesto dotted-note rhythm, and a forewarning of the buried trill by the *appoggiatura* for an inner G-sharp on the first beat of measure five. The very words of its heading are *important: Tema*, the model's musical substance which contains the essential nature of the work; *quasi*, only the suggestion of a resemblance, which is typical of Schumann's interpretative feeling: *marcia funebre*, the mood at a moment in life caused by a supernatural influence. This six-page manuscript contains working techniques as in the "Five Zwickau Sketchbooks," namely, individual fragments, fleeting thoughts, first sketches, as well as a projected overall schematic plan. Unfortunately, source material for Etudes (1st. ed.): III (Vivace); VII (Allegro molto); VIII (sempre marcatissimo); IX (Presto possibile); and XI (G-sharp minor), is either lost or unavailable. Evidentially, for these five studies, Schumann's inspiration was freshened.

PLATE 4

R. Schumann, manuscript of a further development of the Theme, Opus 13.[8] This essential manuscript is significant because it is the most comprehensive of today's known research material for Opus 13. In a very fair hand it demonstrates the testing and gradual unfolding of Schumann's imagination and taste. Its twelve numbered pages contain ten "Variations" and an incomplete twelve-measure sketch. The heading for these, "Var.," is stricken and numbering is substituted in a revision of the general plan. In addition there are six more pages (unnumbered) for the first appearance of the ultimate *Finale*, dated at its conclusion "Fine 18 Januar 1835." Only the *Finale* shows detailed expression markings such as phrasing, dynamics, gradations of sound, touch, and pedal. The inscription for the entire work reads: "Fantaisies et Finale sur un thême de M. le Baron de Fricken, composées p. l. Pfte et dediées à Madame la Baronne de Fricken, née Comtesse de Zedtwitz. par R. Schumann. Oeuvre 9 [sic]." "Variations pathétiques," which would suggest grief, is stricken. The "Thême" retains the *alla breve* and gives "Adagio" for heading. The grace-note lengths are altered. With subtlety the augmentation of the dotted-note rhythmic figure introduces the opening of the second section. In continuing the melodic motion the opening is given more plasticity and there is no interruption in establishing the *Stimmung*. (In both editions, at the theme's close, the same technic is to be found.)

for that purpose. In truth, Variations 1, 4, and 5 are not orchestral in conception. It would be contrary to his ultimate judgment to scatter these treasures throughout the work. Ranging extensively over the keyboard, Variation 1 is a delicate harmonic painting with the bass tracing lines drawn from the chordal melodic motif. Variation 2, at the fifth measure, is marked "alla fantasia" in the original autograph manuscript. Remarkably, this in feeling and intent is like the fantasy-like section in the Andantino movement of Schubert's *Sonata in A major*, D. V. 959. There is no evidence that Variation 3 should be played fast and energetically as heard today, since Schumann gave no tempo or metronome markings, and it opens with an expressive *Fp*. Rather, it has the character of a dialogue-duet with a suggestion of appoggiaturas slightly shading the interior melodic chordal figure used in the triplet accompaniment. The scrupulously notated rhythm of the top voice also precludes the usual performance. Variation 4 is strongly suggestive of a Chopin *Mazurka*. Schumann must have been loath to part with Variation 5, since he tried to include it in the total scheme in one of the manuscripts.[9] Enharmonically in D-flat major, this transcendent variation, with its wide keyboard spacing and long floating lines, might have been designed as an "Epitaph," giving the final answer to the "Tema, quasi marcia funebre." *Requiescat in pace*. After its close there is added (forte) a simple plagal cadence which seems to have no other explanation. Here is no *diabolus in musica*.

In the beginning of his extensive foreword to Opus 3, Schumann advised the player to dare to explore imaginative use of color drawn from qualities of sound inherent in other instruments. Both this preface and the notation (with given fingerings) of the "Caprices" which follow reveal much of his thinking regarding "taste" and variety in the "execution of embellishments."[10]

For the arpeggio the notation is clear. In the "Theme" the rippled symbol and the tied grace notes placed after the bar are used. Throughout his writing—particularly for appoggiaturas—Schumann is meticulous in placing the symbol before or after the bar whenever possible. The series of melodic notes, falling undisturbed on the beats, demands the first arpeggiations to be slightly anticipatory. (Extremes are to be avoided.) The other example opens out into a sustained chord, melodically spreading from the first note, which coincides with the beat, where the inner tension lies. The rhythmic motif, inserted at the close into E major in the second edition, confirms this.

The solution for the shrouded trill is a matter of taste. Since the principal pedal-point, G-sharp, succeeds a same note, in spite of the aforementioned "appoggiatura," it would be smoother to play the grace note inconspicuously and lightly as a very slight anticipation, merely sounding it enough to quicken the ear.

A less understood problem is Schumann's use of low bass notes resulting in chords or unisons of extreme stretch in the left hand. In this, the probable influence of the historically controversial figure, Abt Georg Joseph Vogler (1749-1814) is a fascinating study. In 1838 Schumann wrote of the lack of appreciation of his compositions. A great teacher (C. M. von Weber was one of his pupils), an organist, and builder of organs, Vogler was supposed to have excelled in harmony. His development of mutation stops enjoyed great favor as an addition to or a substitution for the thirty-two foot stop—the *Quint*.[11] It would be better to play the low bass note A, the Fundamental, in measures six and fourteen of the Theme, simultaneously with the chord. The left hand should then *blend* the added fifth, as an overtone, into the sound. To play the bass note before the beat would make the rhythm at the climax redundant. There are many examples of this throughout Schumann's pianoforte works. Often he notated this as a grace note but meant it to firmly function as a fundamental tone.

The final problems, of slurs and meter, are unique to the Theme of the Symphonic Studies. The use of the slur in piano compositions underwent many changes during the nineteenth century. Its meaning for *phrasing* was not settled by Brahms in his last compositions for piano solo, the *Vier Klavierstücke*, Opus 119. Schumann, experimenting with its usage, may have been the first composer to indicate a phrase by covering a rest. In both editions, successive pairs of slurs appear in the opening of the theme in a manner contrary to all experience. The paradox is that though this employment appears careless, it was, in fact, deliberate and intentional on Schumann's part. As shown earlier, one's attention should be drawn to the critical opening harmony which is intended for the imaginative ear to set the mood. The position of the first slur does this, while that of the second demands a binding of both into a longer asymmetrically balanced line of 6 plus 9 beats. These slurs indicate neither a breath nor an articulation, but continuity of motion. This is reinforced in the first imprint by the term "legatissimo." The literal quality of the march is, therefore, absorbed into a longer, more plastic continuity of phrase, which has the propulsive rhythm of poetry. Only in the final statement are the paired slurs broken at the climax and the reality orchestrally disclosed. The edition of 1852 contains, for the first phrase of the second section, a revision of slurring. These slurs indicate an outlining of subdued melodic embellishment during slackened rhythmic motion in the harmony. Traditionally (from the treatises), this indicated to him the spirit of improvisation.

The editor of a Critical Edition publication should include the given slurs for the first four measures to be found in the original structure of the Theme (Plate 3). Ideally, all of the available pertinent information with illustrations should be reported in a foreword. If there were an authorized revision, it would be better to present the two versions in their entirety. The general rule in publishing, that primary consideration be given to the authorized revision, does not always hold in Schumann's case. The early thrust of his original creative efforts is sometimes denatured by over-refinement in a later version. Schumann's revised slurring, however, in measures nine and ten for the edition of 1852 should be followed. It is an interpretative aid which today's performing artist would understand.

There can be no specific answer to Schumann's exclusive and enigmatic use of the *alla breve* in the MSS illustrated in Plates 3 and 4 and through the first edition. Historically, its various meanings have caused confusion. Schumann may have been influenced by Quantz's *Essay:* "In *alla breve* time there is . . . in an Adagio Cantabile, a pulse beat for each crotchet; . . ."[12] The "cantabile" melody was given by an amateur flutist, and Plate 4 demonstrates the "Adagio." In the eighteenth century the "alla breve style" might represent the opposite of the "galant style." It does not necessarily represent tempo. The Funeral March in Beethoven's "Eroica" is given a $\frac{2}{4}$ time signature. Schubert, for the third "Impromptu" in G-flat major (D. 899), used "¢♩," meaning four half notes to the measure. Considering, however, the very nature of Schumann himself, one could speculate further. At a time of great youthful assurance and daring, is it possible that he, in this work, faced the creature named in Carnaval: Hypothetically, could the "Alla Breve" signify Oedipus' answer to the Sphinx?

NOTES

1. Thomas Carlyle, *Count Cagliostro*, Flight First (Fraser's Magazine, No. 43, July, 1833). "Thomas Carlyle, Critical and Miscellaneous Essays," Vol. III, p. 249 (Charles Scribner's Sons, 1899).

2. A much needed new translation of some of E. T. A. (W.) Hoffmann's literary works is now available: Selected Writings of E. T. A. Hoffmann, ed. and trans. by Leonard I. Kent and Elizabeth Knight, 2 vols. (Chicago and London: The University of Chicago Press, 1969).

3. Leon Plantinga, *Schumann as Critic* (New Haven and London: Yale University Press, 1967), pp. 87n, 139, 142, 146f.

4. *Schumann, a Symposium* ed. by Gerald Abraham; Ch. II, "The Piano Music," Kathleen Dale, (Oxford University Press, 1952), p. 25.

5. Appendix to: Willi Reich, *The Life and Work of Alban Berg*, trans. Cornelius Cardew, 2nd ed. (London: Thames and Hudson, 1965), p. 205.

6. The only known polished version of the five *Supplementary Variations* is to be found in the Landes- und Stadt-bibliothek, Düsseldorf, Germany. It is signed "C. Schumann, 1877." Antedating this copy are two letters of three pages each, dated May 26 and June 14, 1873, written by Clara Schumann to the publisher, Simrock, urging him to ask Brahms, who had refused *her* request, to write a copy of these five *Variations*. In the second letter, Clara says that she "would not know of a better copy than that made by Brahms, who, in any case, solved the few questionable spots better than anyone could." These are on microfilm in the *Alice Tully Collection*, The Toscanini Memorial Archives in the New York Public Library at Lincoln Center, New York City.

7. Autograph now on microfilm in the *Alice Tully Collection*, The Toscanini Memorial Archives in the New York Public Library at Lincoln Center, New York City. Formerly in the *von der Goltz-Vietinghof Collection.*

8. MS in the Bibliothèque de Château Mariemont, Le Morlanwelz, Belgium.

9. MS copy: Brahms Legacy, Gesellschaft der Musikfreunde, Vienna. In his foreword Brahms states that their publication is based on "a copy with corrections in Schumann's hand." Other than Schumann's corrections, in general, its content is fairly similar to the "Mariemont" MS.

10. The influence on Schumann of Beethoven's usage of ornaments and embellishment would require an article of extensive scope.

11. The combination of a 10 2/3-ft. (the mutation) and a 16-ft. stop, which produced a resultant 32-ft. pitch, was designated as the *Quint.*

12. Johann Joachim Quantz: *On Playing the Flute*. Edited and translated by Edward R. Reilly. (London: Faber and Faber, 1966), p. 286.

CHRONOLOGY*

Pianoforte Works Composed Through 1837 Which are in Authorized Publication
(The Five Zwickau Sketchbooks of 1829-1833 in the
Wiede Collection; [unpublished])

COMPOSED			PUBLISHED	
		(1821. Sebastian Erard patented the double escapement mechanism.)		
		(1825. A. Babcock, Boston, introduced the first cast-iron frame.)		
'29-'30	Op. 1.	THÈME SUR LE NOM ABEGG, varié pour le Pianoforte	Kistner	'31
'29-'32	Op. 2.	PAPILLONS	Kistner	'32
'31	Op. 8.	Allegro	Kistner	'35
'32	Op. 3.	Etudes pour le Pianoforte d'après les Caprices de Paganini avec doigter, exercices préparatifs et avants-propos sur le but que l'editeur s'y propose. (Title also in German.)	Hofmeister	'33
** '32	Op. 4.	Intermezzi, (issued in two parts) ('29-'32. Chopin: Op. 10. Douze grandes Etudes. '33)	Hofmeister	'32
'32-'33	Op. 5.	Impromptus sur une Romance de Clara Wieck	Hofmeister	'33
		Impromptus über ein Thema von Clara Wieck für das Piano Forte. *Revision*	Hofmeister	'50
'32-'34	Op. 7.	Toccata, (original version of 1829: unpublished) ('32-'36. Chopin: Op. 25. Douze Etudes '37)	Hofmeister	'34
'33	Op. 10.	VI Etudes de Concert pour le Pianoforte composées d'après des Caprices de Paganini	Hofmeister	'35
** '33	Op. 22.	Sonate in G-moll (So rasch wie möglich. Scherzo)	B.u.H.	'38
** '33-'35	Op. 11.	Pianoforte-Sonate, Clara zugeeignet von Florestan und Eusebius (fis moll)	Kistner	'36-'38
		Grande Sonate pour le Pianoforte composée et dédié à Mademoiselle Clara Wieck, pianiste de S.M.l'Empereur d'Autriche. *Revision* ('34, April 3. First issue: Neue Zeitschrift für Musik)		'40
'34-'35	Op. 9.	Carnaval. Scènes mignonnes sur quatre notes	B.u.H.	'37
'34-'35	Op. 13.	XII ETUDES SYMPHONIQUES pour le PIANOFORTE Dediées a son ami William Sterndale Bennett à Londres	Haslinger	'37
		ETUDES en forme de VARIATIONS. *Revision*	Schuberth	'52
'35-'36	Op. 14.	Concert sans Orchestre (Sonate in f moll)	Haslinger	'36
		Grande Sonate pour le Pianoforte. *Revision* ('36. Essay on "Etudes": NZfM)	Schuberth	'53
'37	Op. 12.	Phantasiestücke	B.u.H.	'38
'37-('38)	Op. 6.	Davidsbündlertänze (issued in two parts)	Friese	'37-'38
		Davidsbündler, Achtzehn Characterstücke für das Pianoforte. *Revision*	Schuberth	'50-'51

*Some Works in Print:
  1731-'42 J.S. Bach: Clavier-Übung
  1823-'27 Beethoven: Op. 111—Op. 135.
  1827 Schubert: Sonata in G Major, D. 894.

**The songs "Hirtenknabe," "An Anna," and "Im Herbste," composed in 1828, were the source of Schumann's pianoforte transcriptions for "Intermezzo No. 4," "Aria," and "Andantino" in opera 4, 11, and 22, respectively.

14

Spelling and Intention:
A Setting of William Alexander Percy's Lyric
A Sea-Bird (1933) by Irwin Fischer

EDITH BORROFF
STATE UNIVERSITY OF NEW YORK AT BINGHAMTON

From the middle of the nineteenth century to the middle of the twentieth century, chromaticism became more and more vital to musical materials. Among many avenues of approach to chromatic writing, two general types can be distinguished in regard to problems of notation: the use of conventional structures in unconventional juxtapositions and the development of new structures. The second of these, being more radical, has achieved greater attention from theorists, particularly because new procedures were necessitated by them, both in composition and in analysis; in general this avenue led toward total integration within the twelve pitches proposed in equal temperament and away from key-tonality.

But the first, being more conservative, has achieved greater attention from performers and instrumental teachers; in general, this avenue led to new definitions rather than to new bases of composition; it maintained the concept of variable roles for pitches, an inequality which, if not supporting a traditional definition of key-tonality, at least depends upon the notion of one or more tones as central to and definitive within the musical context. Upper and lower dominants were seen as perfect fifths away, upper and lower leading-tones as small and demanding minor seconds away from a center, however temporary. Pitches were therefore open to inflection, and equal temperament remained a compromise of convenience.

Pitch interactions in this concept involved several techniques, among them were: *A*, the dissociation of traditional structures from key-tonality through successions of such sonorities without traditional logic (i.e., non-progression and non-resolution); *B*, the combining of two traditional units to create larger, nontraditional units, such as a six-note chord made out of two triads; *C*, the combining of melodic gestures or cells, each clearly related to a root tone, either in a continuing single line of changing tonal allusion or in a combination of lines that effects an opalescent multireference or a fabric similar to that achieved through integration.

Thus, the two avenues can arrive at very similar musical results, and they share problems of notation (see Ross Lee Finney's "Concerning My *Fantasy in Two Movements*"); but they do not share solutions to these problems, for their divergent views require differing means.

The basic difficulty common to both is, of course, the use of thirty-odd names for twelve piano keys. In any musical concept which stresses centripetal relationships, the difference between, say, C♯ and D♭ is considerable, psychologically for all performers, and physically as well for those singing or using instruments which can alter pitch. Decisions of spelling are made on the basis of several desiderata: *1*, to clarify the pitch organization in regard to root or key; *2*, to set off cells for ready identification; *3*, to make a part easier to think, read, or play; *4*, to facilitate interaction among performers; and *5*, conversely, to make certain gestures obscure or difficult in support of the overall chiaroscuro of a work.

Nowhere are these factors in livelier interaction than in the songs of the second quarter of the twentieth century. The Iowa-born, Chicago-based composer, Irwin Fischer, a master of the second tradition, composed a number of songs in the 1930s, among which is the setting of William Alexander Percy's short lyric, "A Sea-Bird."

The three means of tonal interaction mentioned above (*A*, *B*, and *C*) are all prominent in Fischer's work, culminating in a bitonal *Sym-*

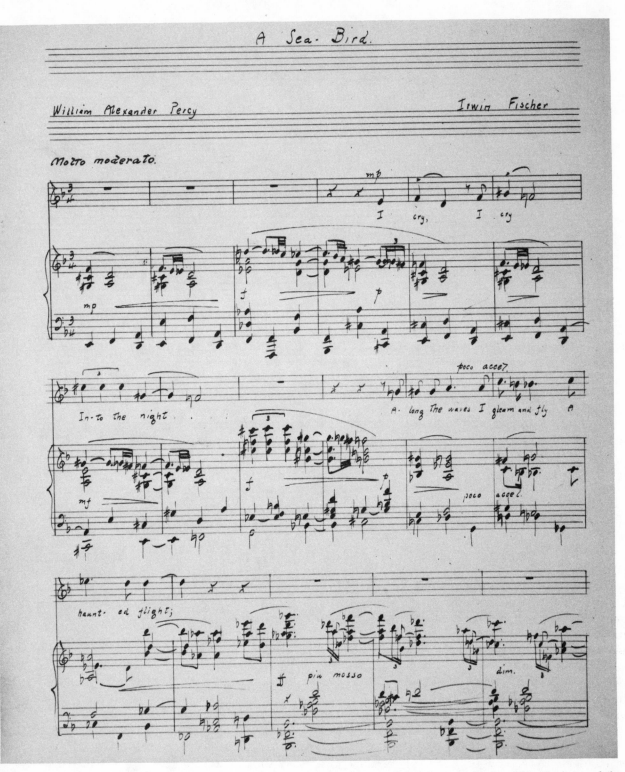

Original copy of "A Sea-Bird" by Irwin Fischer, from the Fairbank Collection of the Newberry Library. With permission of the composer and of the Newberry Library. The poem "A Sea-Bird," from *The Collected Poems of W. A. Percy* copyright by Leroy Pratt Percy. With permission of Alfred A. Knopf, Inc.

phony, which approaches disintegration of tonal allusion through ambivalence. Such ambivalence is foreshadowed in this earlier lyric, combined with certain eastern European characteristics (notably the stressing of both *C♯* and *G♯* as basic to the tonal hegemony of *d* minor) that constitute a personal preference which doubtless was in part what led him to study with Zoltán Kodály. In general, in Fischer's style, dissociated structures (*A*) tend in themselves to be made of two smaller units: (*B*) as an elision, and they tend, in addition, to exploit relationships containing enharmonic whole-tones. His *Concerto for Piano and Orchestra*, for example, combines triads an augmented fourth apart (*E♭*, *G*, *B♭*, *C♯*, *E♮*, *A♮*), a French sound which he uses in a non-French but compelling way. Combining the two major thirds alone (*E♭*, *G*, *A*, *C♯*), though deriving from reference to the two triads, produces the traditional French sixth, itself an ambivalent sonority. Like his use of melodic cells (*C*), Fischer's use of dissociated and combined structures parallels that of many other composers of his own generation, yet in the context of his own style he turns them to a highly individual purpose.

"A Sea-Bird" reflects Fischer's ability to produce a cohesive work with these means, which prove particularly effective in connection with Percy's lyric, which is mystical, uneasy, ambivalent. All five of the desiderata in decisions of spelling (*1* through *5* above) are operative and are of particular interest here because of the combination of voice (pitch flexible) and piano (pitch inflexible) and also because an ambivalence between tonal center and dissociated cells (*1* and *2*) is at the core of meaning in the work both structurally and esthetically.

Clarification of pitch organization in regard to key-tonality (*1*) and cell identity (*2*) are central to decisions, with the importance of *d* minor as a tonal pull primary. The two melodic cells of the song are based upon descending figures related to the "pathogenic" wellspring described by Curt Sachs—certainly appropriate to the text "I cry." The first gesture is a descending minor third, most often preceded by a rising up-beat; this gesture appears in ¾ meter. The second gesture is a descending fourth and third, spanning a minor sixth; this gesture appears in ⅜ meter but is notated as a hemiola figure covering two measures of ¾.

The first figure appears twice at the outset (Example 1).

The second appearance is a tonal answer of the first, modified from the form it would have if the answer were a pure cell (Example 2).

Here the decision has been made to clarify the central position of *d* (in the minor form, with prominent *G♯*).

Likewise, the first appearance of the second cell (measures 7-8) is notated so as to sustain the relationship to *d* (Example 3).

As a pure cell, the second gesture would be notated as a fourth and third (Example 4).

Comparison of the spellings of both gestures as they first appear in the voice with those of the first cell in measures 19-20 and the second at measures 21-23 shows the cells pulling toward their pure form as soon as they are released from the gravitational pull of *d*; measure 37, deriving clearly from measure 7 and choosing db^2 over $c♯^2$ even over a *c♯* bass tone. In these instances the tonal pull is not crucial, and the desire to set off the cells can determine spelling.

Easing performance (3) is a consideration of importance to any practical composer. Fischer chose d^2 instead of the pedantically correct $e\flat\flat^2$ in the top voice at measure 3; in another context, at measure 27, he preferred $d\flat\flat^2$ to c^2, where the correct spelling is not a hazard to the performer. Changes from $e\flat$ to $d\sharp$ at measure 9 and from $g\sharp$ to $a\flat$ at measure 12, both suggested by the composer, stem from the desire to make the keyboard part easier to think and read; the use of cognate spellings or structures in the two hands of a keyboard part is of much greater importance to a pianist than to a composer. Fischer also suggested the clarifying rhythmic change at measure 60.

Facilitation of interaction between performers (4) in a song deals largely in pianistic support. Here the keyboard part doubles the vocal line in a shadow-play of shifting voices, and is of undeniable help to the singer, for whom enharmonic spellings in a tonally-nonintegrated context can be extremely touchy. Although identical spelling is not essential, it helps the pianist to coordinate: at measure 44, $c\flat^1$ would have been preferred in the piano to b, but the pianist joins the singer, for whom the progression from $g\sharp^1$ to $c\flat^2$ would constitute an unnecessary difficulty.

Deliberately obscuring a relationship or making a passage difficult (5) is, of course, exceptional, generally climactic, but can become a powerful factor in such special moments. In this work it occurs notably at measure 37, where the pianist must reach for the ungainly right-hand combination of $d'-f\sharp-c\flat^1$ and the singer must think his entrance in a context including d^1, entering on a $d\flat^1$ over a $c\sharp$ bass—the single such hazard in the piece.

Fischer might well retain the cells today as more vital than the tonal pull, notate the meter as shifting $\frac{3}{4}$ and $\frac{3}{2}$, and present the cadenza-like passage (piano, measures 32-36) as an unmetered interpolation, even using elements of the new notation to give the pianist more freedom.

The editor must decide whether to honor the composer's decisions, made at a time when singers did not think about cells, or to shift to forms he guesses the composer might have preferred had he notated the piece a quarter-century later. Nineteenth-century editors updated the work of their predecessors as a matter of course, but this practice is now frowned upon, and happily so. The decade of the 1930s was part of a transitional time in which traditional notation was being strained but new techniques were not yet defined; it seems better to reflect this straining in an edition than to resolve it. Nor is it wise to opt against the tonal base, even though the music strains against it. For this tonal base in Fischer's "A Sea-Bird" provides an essential dimension, a turning center against which the music can pull and from which it derives and ramifies tension in an effective musical counterpart for the "haunted flight."

A Sea-Bird

William Alexander Percy

Irwin Fischer

lone _____ And the sea is mad _____

Mourn -

- ing, mourn - ing, _____ Bro - ken and strown, _____

_____ It nurs - eth the dead, The dead a - lone And my heart _____

15

Concerning My *Fantasy in Two Movements* (1958)

ROSS LEE FINNEY
THE UNIVERSITY OF MICHIGAN

There are, I think, three steps in the process of composing a piece of music. The first is imagining the work in one's mind. The second is finding the materials or system that can turn the imagined work into an external aural experience. The third is the long process of notating the piece. With publication there is the further necessity of editing.

Composers do not imagine works in their minds in any single way and it would surely be dangerous to generalize about this first step. When I say that I *hear* the work in my mind, I don't mean that I hear it as someone else will hear it after the work is written. For one thing the temporal quality is different—almost lacking or very much foreshortened so that gestures and contours and musical events, though very clear, have something of a spacial quality. These musical qualities are not embodied in notes; I have no vision of the score but rather a sense of the totality of the work. I could quite easily draw a picture or a diagram of the work. A fact that puzzles me utterly is that this image remains in my mind for years until I can get around to bringing it to a musical reality.

The second step doesn't take place until I get into my studio with the intention of composing the work. To find the proper relationship of actual musical notes to my imagined gestures is a very painful process. Improvizing at the piano, drawing pictures at my desk, working with patterns and numbers, doing bits of counterpoint, and, I am told, even whistling, are devices that I use to turn my imagination into a musical reality. My entire musical conscience becomes focused upon the thousands of decisions that must be made and that reflect the values that I hold important. I become obsessed with some system and not always a musically valid one. It is like seeking for a crack in the dam that holds back my imagination and once I have found an opening, I am incapable of questioning its validity. It is this experience, more than any other, that makes me feel helpless in the face of criticism other than my own. It is at this moment that the pleasure of composing is the greatest, for a new world of meaning seems to have been discovered and one rushes to mold the work with the means at hand.

The process of notation springs from the union of imagination and system, the first two steps, and is rooted in the culturation of the composer. A few composers have been able to imagine the printed page, but I am not one of them. The process of notation is more complex for me than just writing down pitches: it also involves keeping in mind the space-time dimension of my original image. It is as though my music had to flow into a matrix. The realism of the performance situation is ever-present in my mind. How will the conductor dramatize the temporal plan? I swing my arms imagining that I am a conductor. How will the strings bow the notes I have written? My right arm goes to work. How will the wind instruments articulate what I have written? My lips and breath attempt to show me. How will the percussion use their sticks or hands? I am concerned with all aspects of a performance and when the work is finished, it is, for me, a performance.

Let me illustrate these three steps in a specific work, my FANTASY IN TWO MOVEMENTS (Ed. Peters No. 6063) for solo violin that Yehudi Menuhin commissioned in October of 1957. Mr. Menuhin scheduled the premiere for June 1, 1958 and had to have the completed score by February, 1958. Had it not been for the fact that the first two steps in the composing of this work had already taken place, I could not have accepted the commission. I was able to get the first half of the work to the performer by December. Mr. Menuhin must have thought that I composed very rapidly indeed. The truth is the opposite. By chance I had conceived of the work years before and had actually found the note pattern or system that was to transform my imagination into a musical reality. All I had left to do was to find time in my studio to write the piece, which is hard enough in itself.

To describe the image of the work that I had in my mind when I composed my FANTASY will depend on my memory. A scholar seeking to understand this process must examine either the random remarks of the composer for some hint or look for internal evidence within the music itself, using perhaps such a device as the Schenker chart. Any analytical chart is like a computer: "garbage in, garbage out." However inadequate these methods, they form the best scholarly source there is. A casual remark by a composer may be very illuminating, like the following from an interview of Elliott Carter in the Sunday *New York Times* of February 1, 1970, concerning his new CONCERTO FOR ORCHESTRA: "I regard my scores as scenarios—auditory scenarios—for performers to act out with their instruments, dramatizing the players as individuals and as participants in the ensemble." And elsewhere in speaking of St. John Perse's "Vents" which triggered the work, he says that "it attracted me by its expansive, almost Whitmanesque descriptions of a United States constantly swept by forces like winds, forces that are always transforming, remolding, or obliterating the past and introducing the fresh and the new." These remarks are in the category of program notes and reflect the first process during which the work forms in the composer's mind.

To return to my own work, there were to be two panels—each a musical arch—the second to be the opposite of the first. I heard the first starting on a pitch in middle range that was to be the focus of the piece; by variations the arch was to rise to its high point and gradually fall back to the central pitch. I heard the phrase gestures beginning short and gradually expanding until the longest and most intense segment was reached and then gradually shortening to the end; the intensity, however, that had been reached must be preserved until the end to justify the second panel. The high and low points were dictated by the violin, but I wished to limit somewhat the high point so that it might be exceeded at the very end of the second panel, and also to avoid too much emphasis of the low G so

that it could also be given greater emphasis later. I wanted the first panel to be more simple, more traditional than the second, so that there could be a feeling of expansion and growth.

The second panel was to start higher and with great intensity. The phrases were to be much less segmented and longer, almost sectional. The intensity of the first section was to dissolve into a humorous section after which a third section would be even more intense. The middle of the movement was to be a slow and singing section that would break, somehow, the confining restrictions of the piece. After this relief or contrast, I heard the first three sections returning in a retrograde order, and the whole piece would be ended by a brilliant coda leading to the original theme of the first movement but having the greatest intensity and the highest pitch point of the work.

The preceding is a description (a memory) of what was in my mind before I had written or heard a note of music. It wouldn't be difficult to draw a picture of this image nor is it hard to realize that this conception could be kept in my mind, as it had been, for a long period of time. However important this conception, it wasn't music, though it did suggest the kind of sound to be sought and the way in which the music would be shaped.

The second step in composing is both the most exasperating and at the end the most exhilarating. It is the most personal, since here the composer reveals his convictions concerning his craft—his attitudes toward traditional technics such as counterpoint, or contemporary technics such as serialization or electronics. The composer has to make a breakthrough, to translate abstract ideas into specific musical patterns. Roberto Gerhard once spoke of the composer's making a "small capital investment" that paid good dividends. Not all composers make the same investment, some fall back on the customs of their culture. Even if the composer could remember the "investment" he had made to turn abstract thought into music, he would hesitate to admit it, fearing that prejudice would be formed which would impair the listening process once the piece was finished. But the composer often does remember, and that memory is a most valuable source for the musicologist. It isn't necessary that the composer *justify* the system he uses in selecting notes—his "capital investment,"—since the only justification is the completed work.

With the image of the piece that I had in my mind and with an understanding of my own musical prejudices and background, I knew what I was looking for. What I didn't know was how or when it would arrive or what kind of work would help me in its conception. I knew it would be based on a 12-tone row that was divided into two symmetrical hexachords. I knew it would have a pitch focus. I hoped that the hexachord could be compressed within a narrow pitch space so that the order of the notes within the hexachord could be free without destroying the formative value of pitch serialization. In other words, I hoped that the associative cohesion (somewhat related to the idea of combinatoriality) would not be lost by the ear, and the opportunities for variety and contrast would be increased.

There is a big difference between a musical idea and a theoretical conviction. It would be easy enough to select a 12-tone row to fit all my requirements but if it didn't generate music—"pay dividends"—it wouldn't be worth much. Perhaps that is the reason why I have never been able to make a breakthrough in this second stage on the basis of theory but have had to seek through improvization for a musical phrase or theme. When it finally arrives, after many have been discarded, I know immediately that it is right and I proceed from that sense of rightness to an understanding of how it has been formed. The following theme came to my mind and ended the period of exasperation:

When I began to analyze how this idea was formed, I found that it was even more simple than I had expected, for there was not only symmetry between hexachords but also within the hexachord. To base a work on a note organization made up

entirely of major and minor seconds seemed almost too rigorous, but the limitations are not as real as they seem, for one has not only octave displacements but many other ways of bringing about interval variety.

The compressed form of the row certainly fitted my demand and it would be hard to think of a simpler beginning for variations. There was even a chaconne-like quality to the theme that would make expansion of vocabulary and of phrase-lengths effective. The scale-wise possibilities were infinite and would fit my idea of violin articulation.

It was at this point that the work stood when Mr. Menuhin gave me his commission. It took me two months to notate the first movement and a month and a half the second. I have forgotten the thousands of decisions that led to the final continuity of the work. Any analysis that I could make now would depend upon the finished score and have no special validity. I do remember that the fugal section at measure 134 seemed to me the right kind of mid-movement tension, not only because of the notes but also because of the

demands it places on the performer. I was also aware of not dissipating the tension too rapidly before the movement ended on D with the simple statement of the theme.

A point that no one else could know about the second movement is the fact that I had to abandon my original start after having worked on it for several days. That original version became, five years later, the start of my SONATA QUASI UNA FANTASIA for piano (Ed. Peters No. 6831). It didn't fit the needs of the violin work for two reasons: a chord resolution problem was inherent and its solution would have destroyed the image of the work that I had in my mind; and second, the scale-wise movement was not an adequate contrast to the first movement and failed to introduce immediately the note-order changes that I intended to exploit. The first panel, "Statement and Variation," uses overlappings and associative juxtapositions from various transpositions of the row to gain a more flexible continuity. The second panel, "Development and Conclusion," uses change of order within the hexachord as can be easily seen in measures 6 and 7. The problem of the slow section in the middle of the movement demanded a more drastic device to destroy the hexachordal symmetry and produce a lyric contour.

I was fully aware of the need to reestablish the pitch polarity of D in the coda (measure 180) and to give the violinist the opportunity of a brilliant ending. The emphasis that I gave low G in measures 50-56, 118-128, and 163-166 and the arrival of the high point D reached in measures 222, 229, and 236 were consciously planned.

When a work is published, there is a last stage of editing and revising where changes of notation may enormously add to the final product, though not usually altering the original creative concept. One must not generalize about this final stage because with some composers, like Mozart, it hardly exists, while with others it is fundamental; with one work of a composer it may take years and involve changes that are creative and basic, while with another work it is unimportant. There is little mystery about such revision; all the scholar needs to do is to compare the printed version with the composer's sketch. The scholar's conclusions about why the changes were made may be more meaningful than anything the composer might say.

The first two pages of my original pencil sketch of the FANTASY IN TWO MOVEMENTS (Plates I and II, property of the Library of Congress) will suffice to illustrate this final stage, though changes were also made in the ink copy (mastersheets) which was submitted to the publisher and on which Dr. Fritz Oberdoerffer, the distinguished orthographer for Peters Corporation, had carefully made his suggestions for proper notation, and Yehudi Menuhin had added fingerings and bowings and interpretive suggestions such as "misterioso senza rigore" in measure 30.

My first change is in measure 4 where A sharp is changed to B flat—obviously to keep the row line more clear. The most fundamental change is mensural and affects measures 29-36 and 40-47. These changes were made for two reasons: they are easier to read when kept in simple measure more consistent with the whole movement, and they result in a more flexible and interesting rhythm in performance. None of the changes made by Dr. Oberdoerffer, Yehudi Menuhin, or myself have changed the work as it originally came to my mind, but they have facilitated the performance of the work and are, therefore, of great importance. They must not be confused with the revisions that took place during the creative process of composing the work.

Few composers like to admit the thought and the hard work involved in writing music because there is a popular idea inherited from the nineteenth century that art is spontaneous and uncontaminated by the mind. No composer likes to write program notes because he feels his job ended with the notation of the score, nor does he like to talk about his music while he is in the process of writing it. Even if a critic or a scholar writes about his music in a way that he feels is untrue, he prefers to remain silent, for the work is done and he is no longer involved with it.

Ross Lee Finney: Sketches for the Fantasy in Two Movements, from the Library of Congress. (Peters Edition No. 6063). Copyright 1958 by Henmar Press Inc., sole selling agents C. F. Peters Corporation, 373 Park Avenue South, New York, New York 10016. Reprinted with permission of the publishers.

6
Moderato ♩= ca. 72 (♪ are equal)
pesante
a tempo
f marcato
cresc.
ff pesante
ritenuto
fff
Peters Edition No. 6063

7
Presto ♩= 72 - 80
pp leggiero
cresc.
mp
mf
rit. e cresc.
A tempo ♪ sempre eguale
poco a poco cresc.
Peters Edition No. 6063

8
Maestoso ♩= ca. 72
meno mosso
calando
molto
Teneramente ♩= ca. 40
p freely
un poco rit.
len.
Peters Edition No. 6063

9
len.
mp
cresc.
rit.
poco
a - poco - ritardando
pp
Tempo primo ♩= ca. 66
sf
dim.
Peters Edition No. 6063

14
rit.
Presto ♩=ca. 152
cresc.
poco a poco cresc.
p sub.
Peters Edition No. 6063

15
mp sub.
con fuoco
allargando ma più marcato
pesante
Peters Edition No. 6063

16

A New Notation:
Soliloquies for Violin and Piano (1971)
by Paul Cooper

EDITH BORROFF

STATE UNIVERSITY OF NEW YORK AT BINGHAMTON

Throughout the early decades of the twentieth century composers have expanded the scope of sounds and techniques they demand of performers. By 1960 so many scores included new elements of notation that theorists were beginning to speak of a "new notation" and of the "new music," a term which has a long and interesting history. In 1966 the Hermann Moeck Verlag published Erhard Karkoschka's extended study of new forms as *Das Schriftbild der Neuen Musik*, "the graphic notation (literally, picture-writing) of the new music."

Like other innovations, new notation maintains much of the old: staff-lines, noteheads, stems, bars, accidentals, attack and expressive markings—all are available for use and retain their traditional meanings without their traditional obligations. But in addition, new signs are added. Of these, some, such as the indication for piano clusters (see II of the Cooper *Soliloquies*) have been standard for a generation or more. Others, such as Cooper's indication of preparation of a piano with 1/8″ bolts (see VI), are devised by composers as they are needed; those which are needed frequently and become widely utilized will enter the system. Other techniques use old signs in new ways, such as the solid notehead without stem to indicate notes of unspecified duration but quicker than open—whole-note—heads (see I).

New techniques and signs serve to designate demands in three categories common to all notations: rhythm, pitch, and instrumental technique. In all cases, they simplify. It is possible to write clusters out in full, for example, but they are difficult to read (though they are easy to play) and deflect the attention of the performer to matters not essential to the musical meaning.

The Paul Cooper *Soliloquies for Violin and Piano*, composed for this volume and dedicated to Louise Cuyler, include new notation techniques in all three categories. It is an essentially lyric set, and requires no percussive effects from either player, concentrating on more traditional pitch and technical demands in the violin part and softer effects in the piano part. Typical for works using notation of an innovative sort, the composer has included instructions on the meanings of new signs.

Rhythmic approximation through spacing of signs rather than by their individual detail of appearance is probably the most conspicuous of the new techniques of notation in the *Soliloquies*. Such notation seeks rhythmic spontaneity and direct interaction of the players, who must listen to each other rather than to the metronome. Such effects can, of course, be notated by being carefully set in intricate, metrically precise notations. But such full notation serves not only to complicate a basically simple effect, but it forces the performers to concentrate on just those elements from which the composer wishes to free them. The opening notes of I, for example, can be written in traditional notation (though without offering the options of rhythmic detail that is central to the goals of new notation):

Here the performers must count precisely, focus upon metrical accuracy to produce an effect of metrical freedom—or disregard the metrical element and proceed freely as though the notation were as Cooper wrote it. Cooper's solution is much simpler, much more natural, much more consonant with the musical meaning, and much easier to think and read. In addition it reflects the desired rhythm in a spacious and esthetically pleasing visual effect.

The new symbols—notably the clusters in II and the triangular and diamond-shaped noteheads in IV—are not available on the musicwriter used by many music inscribers. Those who use stencils can cut new forms, but type fonts or musicwriter keys do not yet include them. In this case, the edition represents a collaboration between inscriber and artist; such collaboration underscores both the esthetic quality of the notation and the central importance of the editor, who is the only worker to see the notation whole.

Aside from the piano clusters in II, quarter-tones for the violin form the primary pitch modernism of that part, and, like the cluster, the quarter-tone has a long familiarity. Both are instrumental techniques associated with only one of the instruments in the *Soliloquies*, and cannot be exchanged with the other—i.e. the piano cannot produce quarter-tones and the violin cannot manage twelve-note clusters. The same is true of violin harmonics (one of the traditional techniques Cooper uses—in IV) and the striking or strumming of piano strings inside the body. Silent cluster and prepared piano elements are perhaps the most all-encompassing designations, including rhythmic, pitch, and qualitative elements. The directive for piano quality at the opening of I, for example, cannot be notated in traditional terms. The symbol for striking with the thumb and the second and third fingers (in V) uses the stem, flag, and tremolo slashes of traditional notation, but its new look incorporates pitch direction, rhythmic suggestion by spacing and by ties into space (one of the earliest of the century's new symbols), and pianistic effects that demonstrate the extent to which new ideals have made their way into the daily life of music.

to louise cuyler

S O L I L O Q U I E S

FOR VIOLIN & PIANO

a) dampen notes with l.h. inside piano
b) play on keyboard, free rhythms
c) 1/4 tones, up and down, becoming wide vibrato

Soliloquies for Violin and Piano by Paul Cooper. With permission of J. & W. Chester Ltd., London, Publishers.

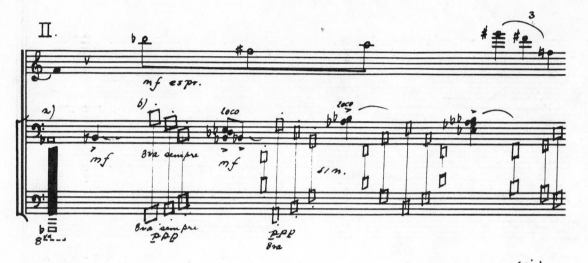

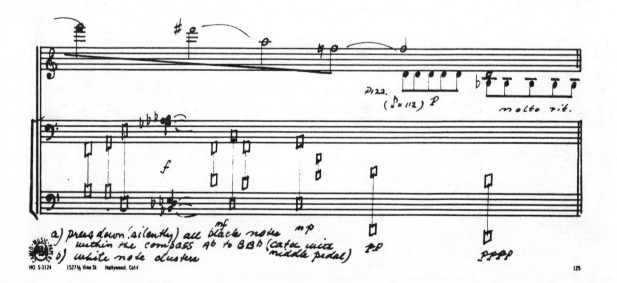

a) press down (silently) all black notes
   within the compass Ab to BBb (catch with middle pedal)
b) white note clusters

a) repeat as bell tones

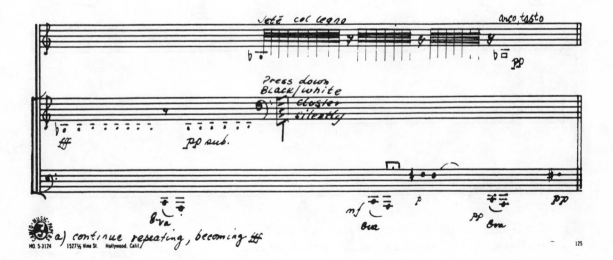

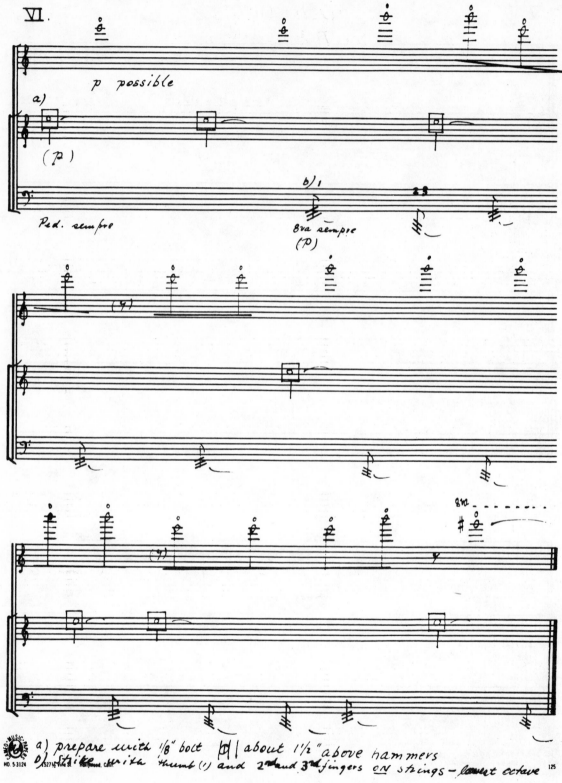

a) prepare with 1/8" bolt d) about 1 1/2" above hammers
b) strike with thumb (1) and 2nd and 3rd fingers ON strings — lowest octave

To Louise Cuyler
SOLILOQUIES
for Violin and Piano

Paul Cooper
1972

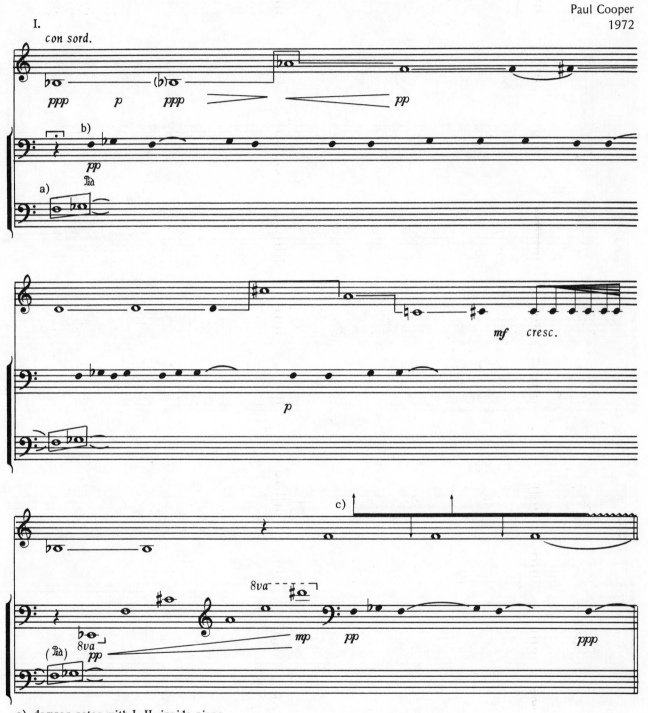

a) dampen notes with L.H. inside piano
b) play on keyboard, free rhythms
c) ¼ tones, up and down, becoming wide vibrato

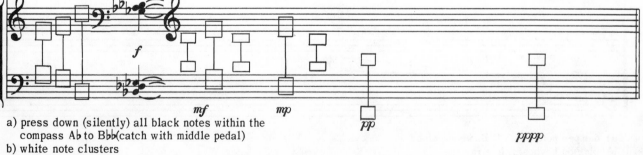

a) press down (silently) all black notes within the
   compass A♭ to B♭♭(catch with middle pedal)
b) white note clusters

III.

a) repeat as bell tones

IV.

a) continue repeating, becoming *fff*

VI.

a) prepare with ⅛" bolt |φ| about 1½" above hammers
b) strike with thumb (1) and 2nd and 3rd fingers <u>on</u> strings – lowest octave